ROCK YOUR CLASS
CREATIVELY IMPACTFUL TEACHER-ROCKSTAR TIPS FROM A TO Z

Rock Your Class: Creatively Impactful Teacher-Rockstar Tips from A to Z
© 2020 by Steven "Étienne" Langlois

All rights reserved. No part of this publication may be reproduced in any form or by any electronic or mechanical means, including information storage and retrieval systems, without permission in writing by the publisher, except by a reviewer who may quote brief passages in a review. For information regarding permission, contact Code Breaker Publishing or visit ww.rockyourclass.com

This book is available at special discounts when purchased in quantity for use as premiums, promotions, or fundraisers or for educational use. For inquiries and details, contact Code Breaker Publishing or visit www.rockyourclass.com

Published by Code Breaker Publishing, Ontario, Canada for www.rockyourclass.com
Cover Design and Photos by Julie Archambault-Morgan
Additional Photos by Étienne fans from around the world (used with permission)
Editing by Ternias Publishing
Paperback ISBN: 978-1-7752480-1-9
Ebook ISBN: 978-1-7752480-2-6
First Printing: MAY 2020

To Kerry: for your love and support, for encouraging me to do what I do, and for helping me become the best version of me.

ALL TEACHERS ARE ROCKSTARS

Teacher-Rockstar (n):

an educator that amplifies student engagement, shakes up learning and can rock curriculum content with creativity.

#rockyourclass      www.rockyourclass.com

FOREWORD

SHAKE UP LEARNING.
AMPLIFY ENGAGEMENT.
ROCK ENROLLMENT.

What is a rockstar's favorite hand in poker?
— A full house

When I first met Étienne 25 years ago, it was, in fact, in front of a full house of enthusiastic (and loud) student fans at a concert at Centennial Hall in London, Ontario for which I had the pleasure of serving as emcee.

My opening question then — and now — is a nod and wink to Étienne's admitted penchant for puns but it is also a tribute to his appeal as a performer. His energy, passion and charisma have led to full house concerts around the world during his twenty-five year plus career as a Rock Star and educator.

Recently, Étienne traded in his musical keyboard (at least temporarily) for the technological kind of keyboard. The product of this exchange is **Rock Your Class: Creatively Impactful Teacher-Rockstar Tips from A to Z**, A full house, in its own right, of tips, tactics, tricks, and strategies for all educators with an interest in motivating students.

As you begin to read this, I think that you will be as grateful as I am that Étienne has moved from his dual identity as educator and Rock Star to become a triple threat by adding author to his persona.

Rock Your Class is a resource for all seasons. As a seasoned educator, myself, I have benefitted from many of the ideas and strategies to refresh my practice and to infuse it with

FOREWORD

SHAKE UP LEARNING.
AMPLIFY ENGAGEMENT.
ROCK ENROLLMENT.

contemporary approaches to teaching and learning. The **Inspector Gadget** chapter encourages us all to integrate technology into our teaching and to acknowledge the important role it plays in our students' lives.

For the beginning educator, it is a wonderful companion and induction into teaching. In it, Étienne illustrates the importance of time-tested, enduring strategies such as **Question Everything** that encourages the teacher to spark the curiosity of students and to place learning in their hands by asking questions to connect the learning with students' lived experiences.

Part "how to" manual, part resource guide, and part "tonic," **Rock Your Class** also advocates for educator self-care and wellbeing. In the chapter **Healthy Teacher-Self**, Étienne offers suggestions and tips to help maintain a healthy work-life harmony for teachers so that our passion, enthusiasm, and stamina endure!

This resource is designed to be used in a variety of ways to suit your pace and needs. Pick it up and read a section that meets a "just in time" need, or take the whole book to your favorite reading chair, the beach or the patio, and dig in.

Add your own flavor or approach to the many strategies and tips, and enjoy rocking your class!

— Dr. Michael Salvatori, Educator and Author

ROCK YOUR CLASS
CREATIVELY IMPACTFUL TEACHER-ROCKSTAR TIPS FROM A-Z

FOREWORD

SHAKE UP LEARNING.
AMPLIFY ENGAGEMENT.
ROCK ENROLLMENT.

WHAT TEACHER-ROCKSTARS ARE SAYING ABOUT
ROCK YOUR CLASS

"Absolutely amazing! There are so many fantastic aspects of this book that I don't know where to begin. This book is chock-full of ready-to-use activities. I love all the QR codes, what a great way to give even more information to the readers. Plus, you are so generous, you are giving away all your templates, music and videos. Teachers will flip when they read this. I will be purchasing many copies to give away to my beginner teachers; especially for the chapter on teacher welfare."
— Diana Boisvert, Resource Centre Director, Canada

"I have been teaching French for almost 20 years and still learned some new ideas! The QR codes linking to files, videos and activities made the book interactive and gave me activities that I can use with my classes today! I feel like I can be a rockstar! The Étienne rockstar stories interwoven with classroom stories were entertaining and show how easy it can be to make small changes in the classroom to make a big impact on student learning and engagement!"
— Dawn Fiorilli, MS teacher, USA

"Reading Étienne's book, I want to teach middle school again."
— David Graham, College Professor, USA

ROCK YOUR CLASS
CREATIVELY IMPACTFUL TEACHER-ROCKSTAR TIPS FROM A-Z

FOREWORD

**SHAKE UP LEARNING.
AMPLIFY ENGAGEMENT.
ROCK ENROLLMENT.**

"You have captured the essentials of being a great teacher. It's all about engagement and allowing students to be the best they can be through a wide variety of strategies and activities. Every student learns differently, and your book provides teachers, new and experienced, with practical, fun and engaging activities that can be incorporated easily into any classroom."
— Mary Edwards, Faculty of Education Student Advisor, Canada

"Funtastic book filled with tips, stories, and ready to use samples that are perfect for new and seasoned teachers of any subject area."
— Marie Premi, ES teacher, Canada

"It doesn't matter what you teach, Steven has 26 great ideas to turn your classroom teaching up to 11! If you want your kids to be rockstar learners, read this book."
— Chris Woods, Teacher, Podcaster, & Author of Daily STEM, USA

"Thank you for your incredible resources, motivation and inspiration!"
— Debra Falkenberg, HS teacher, USA

"Rock Your Class, with its conversational tone and personal anecdotes, is a well-written and entertaining read that will leave teachers with many tools they can use to engage and motivate students — in any grade and in any subject area."
— Sherry Holloway, Author/Educator, Canada

**ROCK YOUR CLASS
CREATIVELY IMPACTFUL TEACHER-ROCKSTAR TIPS FROM A-Z**

FOREWORD

**SHAKE UP LEARNING.
AMPLIFY ENGAGEMENT.
ROCK ENROLLMENT.**

"Rock Your Class is filled with fun and creative lesson ideas and activities with QR codes to videos, worksheets and templates. The ideas in Rock Your Class could be applied to any subject matter and used by new and experienced teachers alike. As an experienced teacher, I was introduced to some new activities as well as reminded about some great ones that I had forgotten! Having been a music teacher, the rockstar-teacher analogy and stories were also entertaining!"
— Alana Padilla, ES, MS and HS teacher, Singapore

"This book should be a mandatory reading at every level because it challenges us to think about best practice, reflect on our own, and encourage growth with our students!"
— Brian Aspinall, Educator and Author

"Wow! That was an incredible read! People are going to LOVE all the amazing lesson ideas and access to free resources. I loved how it felt like a conversation — telling stories and sharing experiences. I genuinely lol'd so many times. This is a must gift for any new or aspiring teacher."
— Hayley Duggan, ES teacher, Canada

"Your craft is better than any textbook or curriculum I've followed. Thank you for all you do to engage students and inspire teachers."
— Diane Traver, HS teacher, USA

**ROCK YOUR CLASS
CREATIVELY IMPACTFUL TEACHER-ROCKSTAR TIPS FROM A-Z**

A TO Z

**SHAKE UP LEARNING.
AMPLIFY ENGAGEMENT.
ROCK ENROLLMENT.**

TABLE OF CONTENTS

I. INTRO	**1**
II. CHAPTERS	
A Lay of the Land	4
Be the Learning	10
Candy Curriculum	17
Drumroll of Tongue	22
Executive Pen Exercise	24
Funny Makes Sunny	29
Guitar Solo	34
Healthy Teacher-Self	37
Inspector Gadget	41
Just Be Positive	46
Keep Up	53
Let Me Spell it Out	58
Mime Time	64
Needs More Art	67
Out The Door	71
Play With Matches	75
Question Everything	79
Routines Root Teens	83
Set the Stage	87
That's a Rap	93
Undercover Agent	98
Violins in the Class	102
Why Oh Why	106
Xpert Help is Here	113
Yuck! Marking!	117
Zest to Compete	121
III. OUTRO	**126**

**ROCK YOUR CLASS
CREATIVELY IMPACTFUL TEACHER-ROCKSTAR TIPS FROM A-Z**

INTRO

SHAKE UP LEARNING.
AMPLIFY ENGAGEMENT.
ROCK ENROLMENT.

Anchorage, Alaska, USA

Growing up, I never wanted to be a teacher; I wanted to be a rockstar. One day, in grade 11 English class, I distinctly remember turning to my friend Shelley and saying, "I swear to God, I will never become a teacher." Not five years later, I was standing in front of my very own class as a teacher. God has a funny sense of humor, I guess.

As fate would have it, the rockstar thing was soon to follow. On a cold February day in 1994, I attended a board-wide French teacher meeting. There, I shared a couple of songs that I had written as a French teacher: songs designed to grab student interest and teach them hard-to-grasp concepts. After playing the two songs, Elaine Marentette (the board French Consultant) said, "We have our very own rockstar here! It's Étienne!" She simply took my name Steven, and translated it to its French equivalent, Étienne. At that moment, I became an accidental rockstar. Countless music videos, resources, multiple sold-out tours in theaters and arenas worldwide, and thirteen albums later... I guess that you can say I live the dual life of a teacher and a rockstar.

So let me formally introduce myselves: I am Steven Langlois, full-time teacher, and Étienne, full-time rockstar.

Wikipedia Bio

TV Network Documentary: "The Accidental Rockstar: Étienne"

Teacher. Rockstar. Is there a difference? Standing in front of thousands of screaming fans in sold-out arenas or standing in front of a packed classroom of students, it's all the same. Teachers and rockstars are both performers. Why else are teachers given performance appraisals? We are often measured by our ability to belt out a tangible teaching tune, a pedagogical pop powerhouse, or a curriculum content crushing classic.

In my career, now spanning four decades, I have picked up enough Teacher-Rockstar tips to fill an entire catalogue. It's my hope that the A-Z tips found in this book will help elevate your Teacher-Rockstar game. In each chapter, I will share a quick story and lay out an applicable teaching strategy or tip that will make a positive impact for you and for students of any age, grade level, or subject area.

I have lived these tips and used these strategies with students from grades K to 12. No matter the age of your students, give these a go. Even try the ones that you may find too "childish" for your older students. Believe me, the day that we relinquish the child in us is the day things start to go downhill.

The parallels between the music world and the teaching profession are many; the crossover is undeniable. Look at this Teacher-Rockstar glossary of just some of the commonalities:

Glossary of Teacher-Rockstar Parallels

```
Teachers = Rockstars          Students = Fanbase
Colleagues = Bandmates        School = Record label
Admin = Tour management       Classroom = Theater
Front of class = Stage        Lesson = Concert
Learning goal = Song          Planning = Songwriting
Teacher voice = Speakers      Curriculum = Music
Years = Tour experience       Parent interviews = Media
Teacher tools = Equipment     Strategy = Chart-topping hit
Unit of study = Album         Field trip = Concert tour
```

When I started presenting keynote addresses and workshop sessions in 1994, I would start by asking three simple questions:

1. Is there something out there that can help my students grasp and never forget important curriculum content?
2. How can I keep up when all my students would rather listen to their loud music and play their addictive video games?
3. Is there an effective way of teaching whereby my students will be begging to stay and learn more?

Fast forward over 25+ years later, those questions are still relevant, as are the answers. This book is the A to Z of outside the box, off the stage and into the classroom Teacher-Rockstar tips that have transformed the way I approach teaching. In terms of teaching strategies and preparation, this is rock 'n' roll meant to rock enrollment. This book is a manifesto designed to amplify student engagement and shake up the classroom to the point where students are living what they're learning.

Get ready to rock your class!

A LAY OF THE LAND

ROCKIN' REASON

Even the physical landscape of a classroom can be used as part of the learning process. Surprise and involve your students in classroom layout changes.

ROCKIN' REQUIREMENTS

- ✓ Desks
- ✓ Chairs
- ✓ Tape
- ✓ Paper
- ✓ Scissors
- ✓ Content questions and answers

GLOSSARY OF TEACHER-ROCKSTAR PARALLELS

Colleagues = Bandmates

Team-teaching can be like performing in a legendary, pedagogical rock band.

I don't often stand still when performing a concert. I love to venture out into the audience and sing along with students and teachers. This means that before a concert, the first thing I do when I arrive at a theater or arena is survey the lay of the land. This is important because no two venues are alike. In Hamilton, New Zealand, I had to perform in a bowl. I danced around at the bottom of the bowl looking up at all the hundreds of faces that surrounded me from all sides. It was unlike anything I had experienced before. You can imagine how different that would be compared to singing from a crowd-facing stage. It would be like a teacher standing in the middle of the classroom with all their students' desks facing directly towards the middle, surrounding the teacher.

That experience helped me greatly when, years later, I arrived for a concert in Thunder Bay, Canada. I was told by the crew that a professional wrestling show had been there the night before. The crew asked me where I wanted my stage to be set up. I looked and saw that the wrestling ring was still standing in the middle of the arena. Childhood fantasy fulfilled! I performed that day in the middle of the ring surrounded by over four thousand fans. Scan the QR code below to witness my WrestleMania moment.

Hamilton, New Zealand

Thunder Bay News coverage of arena show

As a performer, I need to consider where the students will be seated. Where are the aisles? Are there balconies? How can I get to the upper level? Where are the stairwells? Are the stairwell doors locked? That last one is important. Believe me.

On more than one occasion, I have ventured off-stage and into the stairwell only to find myself locked out and forced to use the emergency exit doors. Can you picture it? That's right! More than once, I've had to run outside of the entire theater and back in through the main entrance in order to rejoin my own show. Now, I make certain that all stairwell doors are unlocked before each concert starts, so that I can visit those crazy fans shouting from the balconies above.

My least favorite theatres are the ones with no aisles. Theatres like the Centre in the Square in Kitchener, Ontario. Don't get me wrong, venues like these are beautiful. It's great performing to a packed crowd where everyone is right there in the middle, but then I have to stay onstage. I don't like that. I need to move. I need to connect with my audience.

Packed show at the Centre in the Square, Kitchener, Ontario, Canada

As a teacher, I like to vary the lay of the land. Most teachers stick to the same physical desk setup and change the seating assignments from time to time. I like to completely shake things up. I believe you can use anything as part of the learning process, desks and chairs included. The key is to consider not only "to what" we change the physical setting of the class, but also "how" we change it. Most of the time, my desks are set in rows. Not out of tradition, but rows allow me to springboard many other desk formations into action at a moment's notice.

Here are three desk scenarios that I like to use in my classroom:

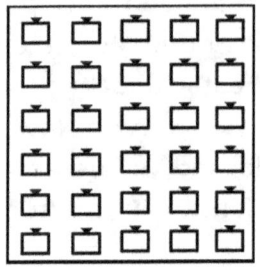
Scenario 1 – Straight rows

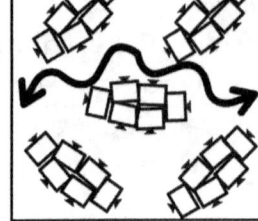
Scenario 2 – Paris

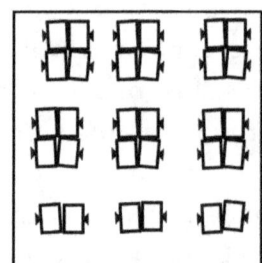
Scenario 3 – Groups and pairs

All three scenarios allow me and my students to move freely around the classroom. This is useful when I'm teaching a lesson or if my students are working in groups.

DISCLAIMER: *I have taught many subject areas, but I have spent most of my career teaching French. Please note that while many of my examples will stem from my experience as a French teacher, the tips and ideas that I share are applicable across all subject areas. Merci.*

The arrows that you see in Scenario 2 represent the river Seine. With my grade 10s, I like to use this setup. Students are grouped into les arrondissements de Paris (Paris neighborhoods). Their first task is to learn about their neighborhood. Grabbing broom sticks, we simulate hanging onto the metro bars of a subway car as the class visits each arrondissement and learns from the dwellers within.

For the rest of the unit, students come into the classroom and the first thing they do is check their mailbox before heading to their arrondissement. In the mailbox is the assignment of the day. One day, they will be searching for an apartment. The next day, they may be shopping for furniture or groceries. The following day might be the task of finding a job. Each task is authentic and always related to where they are and how they are seated.

From any of these scenarios, I can quickly change things around. One of my favorite activities is to hand students a card when they walk into the classroom. They find the corresponding card on a desk and have a related task to complete. Now, I know that many teachers do this to assign new seating for their students, but I like to take things a bit further. After they find their desk, they physically move it to match with another desk or desks.

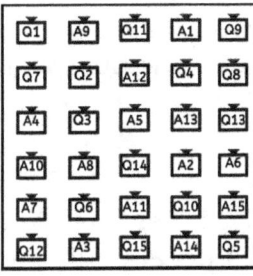 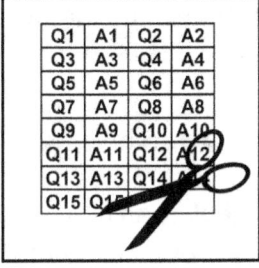 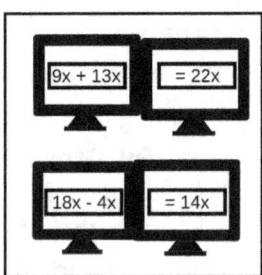

Figure 1. Cards taped to desks   Figure 2. Question/Answer cards   Figure 3. Sample desk pairing

In French, I use this activity to have students match parts of a sentence. For History, I match events with historical figures. In Math, you can have equations and solutions. In Science, you can have problems and solutions. The possibilities are endless.

Best of all, this activity takes just five minutes to prepare. I open a text document and make a grid with 15 questions and 15 corresponding answers. I then print two copies. The first copy, I cut out and randomly tape the questions and answers to individual desks (Figure 1). The second copy, I cut out and randomly hand out the questions and answers to students as they walk in (Figure 2). Students are tasked with finding the desk that matches their card.

Once all students have arrived, they have to figure out a way to reorganize the desks so that the questions are matched with their corresponding answers (Figure 3). Now, if you do not want to have students move desks around, simply do step two and have students find their question-answer match, and then find a random spot to sit together as partners.

Don't have your own classroom? No problem. Even if you are teaching for only 30 minutes in a classroom, you can take the first and last two minutes of a class to rearrange and return desks back to where they were, using drama activities like these:

- **On the Moon:** Desks move in slow motion in this no-gravity zone.
- **Silent Movers:** Desks are boxes filled with precious breakables and there are sleeping babies in the next room.
- **Boxes of Butterflies:** Be gentle with the desks: one bump and out go the butterflies.
- **Nascar Pit Crew:** Time your students.

When I teach the life aspect (unit) called "Suivez mes directions," we change the desks to represent buildings in a city; the rows become streets. We do several navigation activities using our bodies and/or remote-control cars from that setup. Desks can also be arranged to become walls for mazes, with various tasks and challenges added as students work their way through the maze.

However you decide to configure your classroom, use the space you have wisely. When teaching a lesson, keep moving; circle the entire class. If there are students not paying attention, do not stop your lesson. Proximulate: continue teaching while moving closer to those students that are not paying attention.

If space permits, allow for more than just desks and chairs in your classroom:
- Create a quiet corner with special chairs, bean bags, or a rug
- Add a table and an aquarium (fish optional)
- Keep a wooden box for props
- Have a mini bookshelf for subject-related books
- Display student work and inspiring posters on your walls

Whatever you do, remember that, as in the world of the rockstar, the teacher has the power to set the stage. Your classroom is your stage.

BE THE LEARNING

ROCKIN' REASON

What better way to learn course material than by being the course material. Putting learning into action is the way to go. Motion makes memories.

ROCKIN' REQUIREMENTS

- ✓ Music
- ✓ Internet
- ✓ Pens
- ✓ Props
- ✓ Paper
- ✓ Beach balls

Sound technicians at the theaters and arenas where I perform, no matter where I'm at in the world, have all made the same observation: Étienne concerts are loud. Many of my shows reach over 130 decibels. To compare, a jet airplane is 150 decibels. The threshold for pain for the average human ear is about 85 decibels. I remember after one show in Toronto, Canada, the sound technicians told me that my show was louder than the one they had the night before. I asked them who had played the night before. "A band from the UK," they said, "Queen."

But it's not my fault. The sound coming from the guitars, drums, and vocals from my side of the stage is often drowned out by the audio energy coming from the crowd. Short answer? That's right. It's the kids' fault! I believe the reason the concerts are so loud is because, ultimately, the students (fans) want to sing, dance, scream, and have fun. They want to live in the moment. They want to be the concert experience. They want to be. We need to let our students be what we want them to learn.

When I teach Canadian History, I let my students become the history that they are about to learn. Before we even begin the first unit of the textbook, I assign my students the task of looking through the entire textbook to determine who are the thirty most talked about historical figures. Hint: the index at the back of the book is a big help. I provide students with a graphic organizer that has three circles on it (see Figure 1).

After they have determined who the top thirty historical figures are, the top ten names go into the smallest middle circle. The next ten (historical figures #11-20) are recorded in the space provided between the small center circle and the ring of the second circle. The last ten names (#21-30) go in the space provided within the large circle and the second circle.

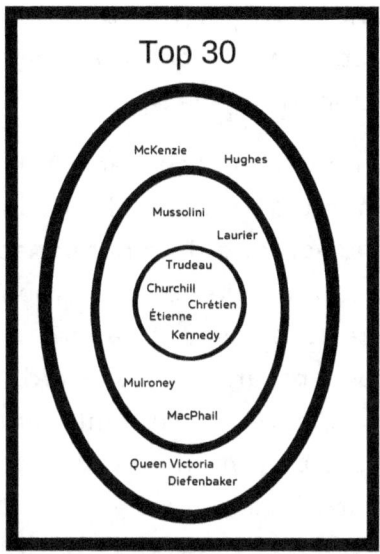

Figure 1. Working sample of the Top 30 Graphic Organizer

To really make things come alive, each of my students choose or are assigned one of those thirty historical figures to research and become. They complete a research organizer tool and learn specific facts about their historical figure. Then, we host a historical figure wine (non-alcoholic) and cheese party in our classroom. Students memorize the facts about their figure, dress up like their figure, and mingle at the party. They are to circulate and meet at least five other historical figures, asking specific questions and recording those answers. Students love the interaction with historical figures from 1900 to 2000. Imagine Churchill, Kennedy, Mulroney, Mussolini, and Queen Elizabeth all socializing together; a true "A-lister" party if there ever was one!

The next day, students have to write a letter called "Dear Mom." In this letter to their mothers, students must write as their historical figure, and detail facts about five interesting people that they met at the historical figures wine and cheese party.

The best part? We haven't even opened up the textbook to start the year and they have already learned more than, I dare say, some students might learn via the traditional way during an entire year. Better yet, I have experts on thirty historical figures that I can go to for support for the rest of the school year.

Another example of how being the learning helped my students was when I exchanged a traditional, tried-and-true teaching strategy with a hands-on one. This happened while teaching a grade 5 unit of common, French classroom vocabulary and prepositions. The previous years, I taught the unit using the French program's accompanying flashcards. I would pick a flashcard from the pile, have the students repeat the vocabulary word that matched the picture, then return the flashcard to the pile. Out of sight, out of mind. Whenever I returned to a flashcard that we had already covered, the students looked at it as if it was the first time they had ever seen that particular flashcard. Results on quizzes and evaluations confirmed that they had learned next to nothing! It was time to shake things up.

I created an electronic dance song that got students not only singing and dancing, but also moving along with the unit's vocabulary in hand. Before the song started, students set up their desks and stood in front of them; like in the image below.

Figure 2. La salle de classe – Desk set-up

When I played the song, they moved in the commanded directions and placed the objects on their desk all around, using the prepositions found in the commands of the song.

Even if you have never learned a word of French in your life, scan the QR code below. I believe that in one viewing, you will understand the power of this hands-on teaching strategy. I guarantee that you will learn at least ten new French words.

Be the learning. To be is a verb. Verbs are action words. If we put action into learning, there is no better way to be pedagogically correct. When adding a physical element to learning, we allow students to become the learning. We know that actions speak louder than words. Get your students active, my fellow Teacher-Rockstars!

Here are two more examples I use in the French classroom, and one you can use with any subject area. The first is a music video that teaches the French verb ALLER using a song and nine easy dance moves. Perfect learning since ALLER is the French verb meaning "to go."

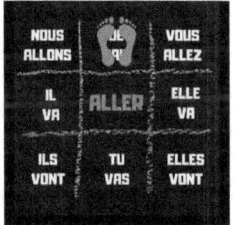 

The second example teaches the French verb AVOIR which means "to have." This music video has students break into groups of four. Students use a beach ball to physically demonstrate having the ball in their hands as they conjugate the verb using the song AVOIR II.

Warning: these songs are very catchy. So catchy, in fact, that even Justin Bieber sang this song live on French national TV.

Back to the small beach ball theme for a moment, here is something that you can do with any grade level or subject area: play educational games using the six colours found on the beach ball. The possibilities are many, but let me provide you with one quick idea. When reviewing a unit of study, create six different categories of questions for the unit, to match the six colours of the beach ball. Here is one example:

Green = Multiple Choice
Red = One Word Answers
White = Define the Term
Orange = True or False
Blue = Identify the Defined Term
Yellow = Spell the Word

When a student catches the ball with two hands, they have to answer a question from the category of the colour where their right thumb rests. Break the class into four teams and play a points-style game.

The possibilities for allowing students to be the learning are limited only by your imagination. Here are some quick ones that you can try with any subject area:

- **Charades:** Have students guess as other students physically act out concepts or keywords from a unit study.
- **Around the World:** One student stands beside another student that is seated at their desk. The teacher asks a speed-round type question. The first student that answers correctly moves on to challenge the next seated student. The student that did not answer correctly first stays seated.
- **Popcorn Reading:** A student stands up and reads orally from a selected text for a few seconds, and then calls out, "Popcorn!" At that time, another random student stands up and reads.

If you walk by a classroom and everyone is quietly taking notes, that does not necessarily mean that they are learning. Too many teachers and administrators are convinced that a good classroom is a quiet classroom.

Students need a balanced approach to learning that most certainly includes hands-on activities. Students need to have active hands. It's like the proverbial broken analog clock: those lifeless hands may be right twice a day, but there is never any real action taking place. Students with idle hands in the classroom might learn a little, but imagine if the hands were moving. Like on that broken clock, when the hands aren't moving, progress in learning stands still.

To sum it up, an inactive classroom is like this broken clock below: both benign (be nine) and ineffective.

CANDY CURRICULUM

ROCKIN' REASON

To mix candy and curriculum content for a deliciously effective learning strategy that will keep your students engaged long after the sugar rush subsides.

ROCKIN' REQUIREMENTS

- ✓ Computer
- ✓ Candy (Skittles™)
- ✓ Paper
- ✓ Microsoft Word or equivalent
- ✓ Game pieces
- ✓ Content questions and answers

Teacher-Rockstars are performers. That's why our administration gives us regular "performance appraisals," right? But how do you rock your performance appraisal? How do you make a lasting impression that will leave your administration writing comments like, "Best teacher I have seen in my entire career!"?

This is my go-to recommendation for performance appraisals. Success is as simple as playing with Skittles™. The object of the Skittles Activity is quite simple: students have the Skittles Activity tool (which looks like a Bingo card) in front of them, along with a handful of Skittles (at least ten). The teacher then asks questions. For each question, the students must find the corresponding answer on the activity tool and cover it with a Skittle piece. In the end, if all questions are answered correctly, the activity tool is covered with Skittles forming a specific design.

Figure 1. Skittles Letters Tool - Answer Design: A smiley face

STEP 1: Create a Skittles Activity template grid or choose one from the free "Skittles Activity Lesson Plan Pack" included with this book (see Figure 9). You can use the blank boxes to insert curriculum content terms, periodic table elements, numbers, letters, or characters from a novel study (Figure 2). You can also go outside of the typical format of a bingo card and create a map of the world or a continent (Figure 3). The possibilities are endless.

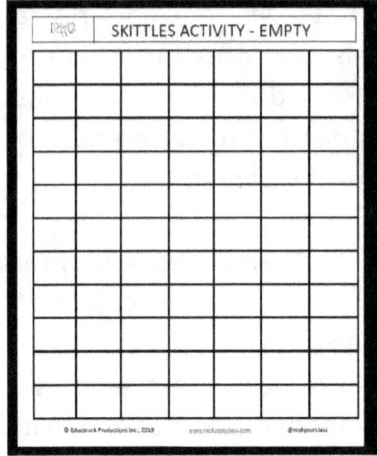

Figure 2. Blank Skittles Activity Template

Figure 3. Skittles Activity Tool - Continent

STEP 2: Grab some Skittles pieces and map out a design. Figure 4 shows a numbers activity tool with the final design of a smiley face. Then, create a script with one question for each of those Skittles covering an answer in your created design. For example, Script 1 in Figure 5 features ten math questions that, when answered correctly, result in students placing their Skittles over the answers on the Skittles Activity number tool that will result in the desired smiley face design. You can ramp up the fun by adding commands like "eat a red skittle."

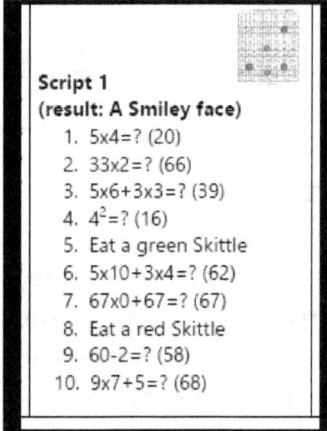

Figure 4. Skittles Number Tool - Answer Design: A smiley face

Figure 5. Skittles Activity Script - Math

STEP 3: Hand out an individual packet of Skittles to each student and have them open the packet, ready to use their Skittles pieces like markers on a hidden treasure map. You can purchase small Skittles packs that contain around ten pieces per pack. If your school or homeschool is candy-free/sugar-free, you can use game pieces, buttons or coins. Remember that game pieces, coins, and buttons are not consumable.

Grab your pre-written script and read each question one by one, allowing students time to think. Once they have figured out the answer, they must look on the corresponding template grid to find that answer and place a Skittle on top of the answer. Once students are ready, ask the next question from your script.

STEP 4: Continue until you have read all the questions found on your script. Circulate the classroom and evaluate the final designs on your students' Skittles Activity tool (grids). You will know if the students have correctly answered all the questions if their template grid bears Skittles that form the desired shape of the script's challenge. You can allow them to eat their Skittles or reuse them for the next scripted challenge.

SKITTLES ACTIVITY - SCIENCE						
H	He	Li	Be	B	C	N
O	F	Ne	Na	Mg	Al	Si
P		Cl	Ar	K		Sc
Ti	V	Cr	Mn	Fe	Co	Ni
Cu	Zn	Ga		Y	Zr	Nb
Ce	Ba	Cs	Xe	Ru	Cd	Pr
W	Os	Ir	U	Pu	Am	Fr
Hg		Au	Ag	Hg		Sm
Cm	Bk			Md	No	
Lr	Rf	Db	Sg	Bh	Hs	Mt
Nd	Te	Sb	I	Mo	Sn	At

Figure 6. Skittles Elements Tool - Answer Design: A smiley face

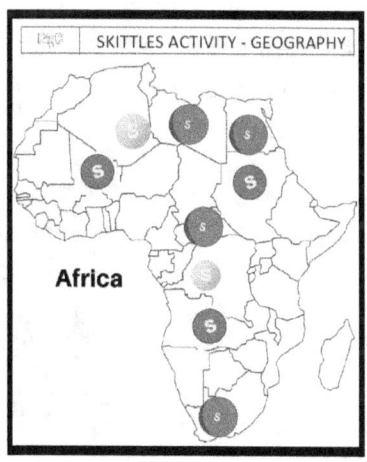

Figure 7. Skittles Continent Tool - Answer Design: Question Mark

STEP 5: Once your students have mastered how to play the Skittles Activity, have them come up with their own scripts to challenge their peers' knowledge on recently learned course content. With the use of a proper template grid, possibilities are limited only by one's imagination.

#	Question, Challenge or Equation	Answer
1		
2		
3		
4		
5		
6		
7		
8		
9		
10		

Result: _____

Figure 8. Sample of the Skittles Activity Script Template

Where there's smoke, there's fire. Where there's candy, there's desire. Many teachers use candy as incentives, and I have seen these incentives work with varying degrees of success. Now we have a learning strategy where we can use candy as the learning tool. Best part? We have another strategy that is effective and not limited to age, grade, level, or subject area. Enjoy the Skittles Activity, my fellow Teacher-Rockstars, as you ace your performance appraisal and rock your class! Scan the QR code below to grab a free download of the entire "Skittles Activity Lesson Plan Package."

DRUMROLL OF TONGUE

ROCKIN' REASON

Alliteration is nature's drumroll of the tongue. It is a memory aid via word-play that leads to smiles, fun, and laughter. Alliteration culminates in cases of curriculum content catchiness.

ROCKIN' REQUIREMENTS

- ✓ Creativity
- ✓ Paper
- ✓ Pen
- ✓ Course content

When our band NOUS (http://nous.band) performs live, the fans love to hear our drummer do a drum solo; he is adept at varying speeds, patterns, and sequences as he bangs away on his drum kit. The crowd claps to his rhythm and he finishes with a phonic fury of fireworks. Drum rolls get a pop out of the crowd every time.

They say a wise person has long ears and a short tongue. Let your students' ears long for learning via short drumrolls of the tongue!

You can add this tip to any daily lesson or visual presentation. To alliterate is to obliterate the ignorance rate. Alliteration is rock and roll for ripping righteous reems of lusciously learned lessons. Alliteration is like ear-candy without the calorie casualties. Take your unit's vocabulary and search for alliteration pairs.

Just as this chapter tip is short, injection of alliteration does not have to be long, but it can awaken some tired minds and bring attention to your intended curriculum coverage. Here are just some examples for different subject areas to give you an idea:

- **Science (Experiments):** Things can **v**ary **v**ery **v**ariably **v**ia **v**iewing **v**ariables through **qu**alitative and **qu**antitative observation, resulting in **c**razy **o**ut**c**omes and **c**on**c**lusions.
- **Geography:** A**l**l **l**ines **l**ongitude and **l**atitude **l**ay across **l**akes and **l**andforms.
- **History: A**rcheologists **a**rrived to **a**rchive **a**ntiquity **a**rtifacts for the **a**nnals.
- **English: C**reating **c**oordinating **c**onjunctions helps **c**onnect, while **c**ommas **c**an **c**ome between two words or parts.

EXECUTIVE PEN EXERCISE

ROCKIN' REASON

To improve pronunciation, enunciation, and presentation proficiency.

ROCKIN' REQUIREMENTS

- ✓ Pen
- ✓ Script
- ✓ Speech
- ✓ Mouth
- ✓ Song
- ✓ Passage of text

GLOSSARY OF TEACHER-ROCKSTAR PARALLELS

A TEACHER VOICE IS LIKE A SET OF SPEAKERS

IT CAN AMPLIFY ENGAGEMENT AND CRANK UP CURRICULUM CONTENT COMPREHENSION

There are various techniques that singers will use to warm up their voices; I use none of them. I have performed two, sometimes three, shows in a day, drank soda between shows, and broken all the other sacred voice-care rules. So, I'm not really one to lecture on this point; however, I've heard that singers are not the only ones that take care of their voices and remain mindful of technique. I have read that Fortune 500 executives do the exact same thing. In fact, one top-secret technique they use before presentations or board meetings is called the "Executive Pen Exercise."

The pen is not only mightier than the sword, it is mightier in the mouth. Looking to have your students completely master their presentation skills, diction, intonation, and pronunciation? Read on, my Teacher-Rockstar friends!

Step 1: Find the perfect script. This may be a section of reading from a textbook or novel that your students are studying, a speech that they are writing, or something more specific. I'll provide you with two specific examples in Step 4.

Step 2: Have students grab a pen and clean it off.

Step 3: Place pen in mouth just behind the eye-teeth (canines). Gently close mouth down on pen.

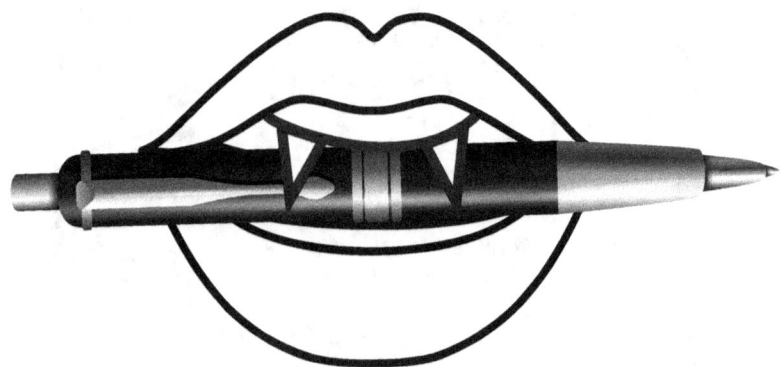

Step 4: With pen firmly in mouth, have students recite the chosen script. If you are looking to target positively perfected pronunciation, look no further than these this little ditty; simply have students repeat after Étienne as the song plays. Tongue Fixters contains a silly, yet effective number of tongue-twisting word combinations to challenge the chops. Scan the QR code (Figure 1) to access the music video. Don't be shy. Feel free to try it with your students or homeschoolers. Note, the phonetic sounds in each double line are designed for students to practice.

Tongue Fixters

[f] [v] For a laugh, savvy Vivian phones her friend Phil
Even Stephen found enough fluffy pillows on the hill
[p] [b] Peter stopped putting peanut butter on the lamb
The baby put the lamp by the purple pepper jam
[t] [d] When Tommy tidied up, did he find my hidden mitt?
Turtles do not dare tread where tigers often sit
[l] [r] Larry read that red leaves are really hard to sell
Murray learned to run his model railroad very well
[s] [z] Six zebra mussels sitting on Sid's lazy nose
Sauce stains are stubborn, as Suzie surely knows
[m][n] No one knows my most memorable memories
Amazing ants are dancing the mambo on my knees
[k] [h] In a quick half an hour I baked a honey cake
I hurt my hands cooking crispy cookies by the lake
[sh] [jz] She usually likes to shop for televisions and machines
My physician has a mission to swim the oceans and the seas
[th] Three thirsty throats thought of something they could drink
But the fact that time was up meant they had to stop and think
[t][dj] Ten joking chickens jumped and stretched on a fridge
Just two of them jumped long enough to cross the ridge
[g] Greg is going to make that thing go bang
Goofy ghosts are singing that great song that Gary sang

Figure 1. Scan this QR code to access the music video for "Tongue Fixters"

Step 5: After students have recited your chosen text, have them remove the pen from their mouth, clean it, and pass it to the student to the right of them. Just kidding! Though, if you are looking to promote community and inclusivity, this may be one way to explore. Again, kidding.

Step 6: With the pen now out of their mouths, have them immediately repeat the script or song. Your head will snap back at how much clearer and more precise their speaking has become with this executives' trick.

Step 7: Encourage students to do this at home in front of a mirror with their toothbrush, or at school with a pen before any major presentation. This technique can be applicable for a lifetime. You can do the "Executive Pen Exercise" to practice a script before an important interview, school or work presentation, or before proposing to the love of your life.

When choosing the perfect script, you can use poetry, prose, or a list of content vocabulary. Whether it be Science, Math, History, Geography, English, or any other subject area, this can be used with any age, grade, or level.

This is a particularly effective strategy with students learning English as a second language. If you teach French, I highly suggest trying this activity using the song "Prononcez-les bien !" You can do a search on any online video platform to find it.

Don't get all shy on me. Maybe you're thinking that you don't want to "die from embarrassment" in front of your students trying out the "Executive Pen Exercise." Let me encourage you, my Teacher-Rockstar friends! You're much more likely to die from a paper cut while reading a paperback novel. Your students will greatly respect that you are trying this learning strategy with them. It's a team concept.

As a singer, I need my microphone; it helps me be heard. I dare say that "The Executive Pen Exercise" teaches us that the pen is mightier than the microphone because it can be used to allow your students to be heard even better.

FUNNY MAKES SUNNY

ROCKIN' REASON

Shed some light on your subject area with some course content related humor. Funny can be the glue that allows key terms or concepts to stick in students' minds.

ROCKIN' REQUIREMENTS

- ✓ Desired lesson content
- ✓ A basic sense of humor
- ✓ Ability to tell a simple joke
- ✓ Comic strip app
- ✓ Computer/Internet
- ✓ Paper/Pen

It was October of my third year as a teacher, and I was teaching the French verb AVOIR to my grade 7 French students. I introduced the song "Avoir II" to them. The students sang the chorus at the top of their lungs. People sleeping from the night shift in the houses nearby could probably hear us. I know the grade 8 English teacher from across the hall did. As soon as we were done singing for the third time, my classroom door opened.

You see, I had always kept the door shut out of respect. Suddenly, the door swung open as thirty grade 8 students and their teacher came walking into the classroom. Without saying a word they stood around us with scowls on their faces and arms folded. I thought I had really done it this time. The English teacher was probably mid-lesson, and our singing ruined everything. To make matters worse, my grade 7s were petrified. We taught at a senior elementary school with five grade 7 classes and five grade 8 classes; there was a pecking order. Grade 7s feared the grade 8s. It was their school, after all. The grade 7s were the newbies, and we were only 40 days into the school year. Now, my twenty-five grade 7s were surrounded by giants.

After an awkward five seconds of silence that seemed more like an eternity, the grade 8 teacher said "Go!" Her grade 8s promptly burst out into singing the chorus to that same "Avoir II" song. When they were done, the largest of the grade 8 boys said in his deep voice, "That's how you sing it!" They all folded their arms again, walked out of my class, and shut the door behind them. After another ten seconds of shock and silence, my entire class and I burst out laughing. It was the coolest thing we had ever experienced. The best part of that experience: my students will never forget the verb AVOIR because of that funny moment.

Most of my memories are tied to funny incidents where we laughed, sometimes until we cried. Usually, that funny moment was triggered by something that someone did or said out of the blue — a spontaneous moment of laughter. After reflecting on the power of funny moments, I began to think of ways to manufacture these moments by carefully creating funny one-liners and stories. This way, we could create memories and make learning stick.

Laughter isn't just the best medicine, you know. Laughter is also the best pedagogical cure for what ails your students. I have always believed that a timely joke or pun can spark laughs and learning, even if you get groans instead of chuckles. I tell my students that once I retire, I'll start my comedy career. My students warn me against the idea, but maybe they just don't recognize comedic genius.

Here are a few original jokes and puns that I've made on my own over the course of my career. Fortunately for all of us, a quick online search can get you much better quality yucks.

These are my top twelve subject-related jokes and puns that I have used with varying amounts of success:

1. **HISTORY:** What WWII era leader was always dragging his feet, never quick to decide? Stalin
2. **FRENCH:** My French friend sees double. He says that every time he sees his father, he sees a 'père.'
3. **ENGLISH:** What did the boy poem say about the girl poem that was sitting on the other side of the room? I can't refrain. I just have to meter.
4. **MATH:** So sad. My friend Isosceles couldn't find the right angle to talk to acute triangle he saw scalene a mountain.

5. **ENGLISH:** Why did the literary term have a bad picnic? He had an antonym the whole time he was trying to eat.
6. **FRENCH:** What are the water levels like in France? L'eau
7. **SCIENCE:** What element is a goofy criminal? Silicon
8. **SCIENCE:** What do elements do with their treasures? Barium.
9. **MATH:** Why can't you do addition while climbing a mountain? I dunno. It just doesn't add up!
10. **GEOGRAPHY:** Why did the cranky geographer have to always have things go his way? He was all latitude.
11. **SCIENCE:** Because students have mass and occupy space, does that mean they matter?
12. **ENGLISH:** E-books are never real page-turners.

I write these on the board or sometimes hand them out on a piece of paper. Then, I read them over with the students to reinforce the key terms found in the jokes. From there, we expand and explore those key terms. So many times, I have heard students commenting on how they remembered a particular term or concept on a test or assignment because of that "dumb joke" or "stupid pun" I had told earlier in the unit study.

It may take you 15 to 30 minutes, but before you start any unit of study, look at the list of key terms and concepts that you want your students to learn. Do any funny jokes or puns come to mind? Write them down. Need more? Use an online search engine and search the keywords "joke" or "pun" and add a term from your course content.

For example, "funny pun photosynthesis" might produce a science joke like this: "I'm not sure what the pigment when he said the hour is lumen, but I don't buy what he cells."

That one, simple science joke covers three key terms in photosynthesis, and can be a catalyst for curriculum content conversation. Humor can turn any dry or hard-to-swallow topic into an exceptional learning aid.

But don't keep the comedic fun to yourself, allow students to do the same. Assign content terms before you begin a unit of study and see if your students can come up with funny fodder. For your visual learners, have your students make memorable memes. You can access several different meme-making apps by doing a simple online search. Memes can be a great way to show knowledge of curriculum content through comedy.

Host a meme or comedy competition using keywords from a current or upcoming unit study. Get your students involved!

Humor is like the sun; it warms the heart and makes students bright. Shine in your classroom by adding humor to the mix of great things you already do to rock your class!

GUITAR SOLO

ROCKIN' REASON

Every rock song needs a guitar solo. It's time for your students to go solo. Give them their moment in the spotlight. Let them take center stage.

ROCKIN' REQUIREMENTS

- ✓ Internet
- ✓ Course content
- ✓ Paper
- ✓ Pen

One tradition that I'm glad I started over 25 years ago is allowing schools to sign up for their favorite songs and have their students dance on stage during concerts. I've always believed that the teachers and students are the true rockstars of the show, and putting students under the spotlight allowed them to shine.

As a result, I have seen some of the most amazingly choreographed dance routines you could ever imagine. While I perform, the students are up onstage under the lights, performing right along with me. Most times, it looks as though we've practiced together, or they're part of the tour. I've witnessed everything from simple dance routines with signs and props to full, hip-hop dance routines and even choreographed ballet.

What students do not know is that I always plan on jumping off the stage and joining the audience, leaving the dancing students under the lights in front of thousands of concert-goers. It's their time to shine and be the rockstars! Without fail, when the song is done, their faces beam as they make their way offstage. Some even don't want to leave!

I love that the students get to shine. I love the smiles on their faces and the sense of accomplishment and stardom.

I've taken this stage tradition and moved it into the classroom. From time to time, I allow my students to become the stars of the show.

You know what they say: if you want to learn something right, you have to learn by doing it yourself. Gradual release of responsibility in life or pedagogy is about giving another individual the opportunity to shine. Let your students rip rad guitar solos once in a while. Allow students to teach or be an integral part of a lesson or class learning opportunity.

Please do not extend this opportunity only to the "good students." Word of advice: if you have students that are disruptive or vying desperately for attention, give them "airtime" and perceived "power." Sometimes, your most disruptive students will excel in these types of positions. Placing otherwise disruptive students in roles of responsibility or perceived responsibility can have a powerfully positive effect. The concept seems almost backwards to instinct, but it can permanently turn a student's outlook. Of course, you would never extend an offer like this at the time of a particular disruption, but you can actually plan a lesson where that student can shine in a positive light. That light-shining experience can be like solar power; it can give them positive energy for weeks to come.

Wondering what kind of roles you could offer your students to allow them to lay down their grand guitar solos? Big and small roles like group leader, timer, teacher of the day, point keeper, peer assessor, and hander-outer are just a few. Remember to allow students to be a part of the planning and defining of whatever roles that you assign them.

HEALTHY TEACHER-SELF

ROCKIN' REASON

Heal thy teacher-self for a healthy teacher-self. Your physical and mental well-being means being pedagogically fit for service.

ROCKIN' REQUIREMENTS

- ✓ Proper rest
- ✓ Proper diet
- ✓ Quiet time
- ✓ Physical exercise

The Teacher-Rockstar life can definitely wear on your mental and physical health. Did you know that I almost had to stop being Étienne right after my third-ever concert? I came home one day to find a 22 page letter in my mailbox. Fan mail, you ask? Not quite. This long letter was from a special-interest group. The letter stated that they were a group of concerned citizens that were responsible for getting popular board games removed from the shelves of retail stores everywhere. The letter outlined how they had successfully tackled giants like the toy company Parker and Gamble, and they explained that I was their next target.

They said that my music and my album (my only one at the time) promoted Satanism and they were determined to stop me. I was 23 years old at the time and I had no idea how to handle a situation like this. Fortunately, it all got sorted out, but it did take a bit of a mental toll at the time.

The lesson of taking care of yourself is one that teachers wait too late into their career to start giving attention. Teaching while being sick or struggling with stress is almost an expected badge of honor that teachers carry into the classroom. Usually, it begins with teachers not taking care of their physical well-being. Not eating properly, not sleeping regularly, not exercising, and never taking time to rest means we can burn the candle at both ends, leading to utter exhaustion and illness.

To break that cycle of self-destruction takes willpower and wisdom. Those were two things I clearly lacked at the beginning of my career. I never took a day off. In fact, I have enough "perfect attendance" letters from education directors to fill a drawer. I was lucky, though. I've spent most of my career eluding serious illness. Well, for most of my life, anyway.

The Teacher-Rockstar life can be deceiving. If you see me driving around town, you may notice that the windows are fully and darkly tinted. Is that to hide from the public and the press? Nope. Doctor's orders. I have a propensity for a reoccurring thing called skin cancer. This is why you will often see me in dark shades, hats, long-sleeve shirts, etc. Why the shades and hats in particular? Let's just say that my skin cancer is written all over my face; coincidentally, it makes it hard for me at times to put my best face forward. For the past two years, I've been getting what I affectionately refer to as my cream-o-therapy. This chemotherapy by cream slowly helped, but if you've seen me on tour any of the past couple of years, you could have found me red-faced and blotchy during one of my treatment cycles. Fortunately, I've been able to schedule most of my live performances and speaking engagements around my treatments. I've had to do at least four or five big shows with a not-so-appealing and a very peeling face, but no one said anything: the press nor the fans. Nothing. I am blessed.

Let's back up and analyse the most important part of this revelation: I had to face the fact that, for too many years, I had neglected a healthy work-life balance for my physical and mental health. In other words, I am guilty of not taking the very advice I'm about to recommend. So, I shouldn't talk, you might think, but on the contrary. I've completely followed this advice since 2017 and benefited greatly.

Now, let's focus on you. What can be more important than your health? You're a teacher. That means that you're most likely a giver. If you're not healthy, you can't give anything to your students. The tips in this chapter are every bit as important as the teaching and learning strategies that you'll find in the others. If you make this chapter your go-to, you'll be able to enjoy the rest of the tips so much more.

Here are my Teacher-Rockstar health hacks and life lifters in terms of maintaining a healthy body and mind:

- Cut out sugar consumption as much as you can to improve your diet.
- Utilise the power of naps. Proper rest is vital to well-being.
- If you've never had a massage, get one. You'll understand.
- There is a reason why schools are not government legislated to run 365 days a year. You are meant to take time off. Take a vacation.
- Pray, meditate, or seek quiet time.
- Be aware of and limit negativity around you. Mindfulness is key.
- Be sure to make time for family and friends. They should be a priority in your life.
- Regularly and increasingly engage in physical exercise.
- Join a group or club of people that share your interests.
- Set goals. Set limits. Stick to your goals. Know your limits.
- Lean on colleagues as they're your pillars for all sorts of needs.
- It's OK to be a bit selfish. Put your health before your students learning needs, which leads to this next piece of advice...
- If excellent resources already exist, there is no need to reinvent the wheel. You don't get extra pay for staying up until 2am creating new resources and lessons.
- Reinvent yourself and your outlook on your professional and personal life.
- Don't take yourself too seriously. Laugh at yourself. Laugh out loud. Laughter is one of the greatest stress relievers.

Not where you want to be health-wise? It's better late than never. In the past two years I've lost 30 pounds. I eat better, exercise regularly, bench press for reps well over my own body weight, and I spend more time with family and less on work. I win and so can you.

INSPECTOR GADGET

ROCKIN' REASON

Times change. We need to change with the times. Use the power of technology to make learning more engaging and relevant for today's students.

ROCKIN' REQUIREMENTS

✓ Computers
✓ Internet access
✓ Electronic devices
✓ Course content
✓ QR scanner
✓ Willingness to learn new technology

Shoes! Shoes! Shoes! It was July and I was doing concerts overseas. My family was with me on tour. One day, my wife and son had plans to visit a cool museum, so my three-year-old daughter was going to hang out with her dad at work. The venue was packed, and the organizer of the concert was onstage introducing me. As soon as I took the mic, the crowd went from applause to a slowly rising chorus of "Shoes! Shoes! Shoes!" I looked out into the audience to see my daughter making her way from the back of the dark theater, up the aisle, and onto the stage where I stood. She wanted to see her daddy. What the audience saw was her new light-up shoes, which hadn't hit their market. This was their first glimpse of shoes that lit up every time you took a step.

Technology: it can amaze us. During concerts, fog machines, flashing lights, and effect pedals are technological tricks to make a live show feel more alive for students. In the classroom, technology can have an equal effect. I'll admit that I have spent parts of my career trying to fight technological advances. I'm an old soul; I like things that I'm used to. Maybe you're like that too?

When it was clear that I was going to become a teacher, I remember thinking to myself, "Well, I guess at least I'll get to play with projector reels." Seriously. I said that several times. Ask anyone that went to Teachers College with me. You see, all throughout elementary school, we begged our teachers to play a movie backwards on the projector machine. No teacher would comply. So, I was determined to do it myself. Unfortunately for me, in my first year of teaching, my school district recalled all reel-to-reel movies because they were putting them onto these new fandangled VHS tapes that were becoming all the rage. Out of rebellion, I grabbed four empty reels and kept them for myself. I still have them to this day.

A lot has changed since I started teaching. When I started out, there were no photocopy machines. No, I'm not kidding. We had what we called ditto machines; you had to fill them with chemicals and run paper through the machine manually. The papers came out hot and the smell of the ink was intoxicating. As a student, I grew up on copies like these in my later school years. Before that, the only way to get copies was to copy things yourself from the chalkboard.

In 2001, iPods and early cellphones made their way into the classroom. You would think it was the end of the world. Many teachers were frustrated with their students and these little music devices. I pride myself on being a problem-solver. So, I thought long and hard about what could be done. You couldn't just take these devices away from students; their empty hands would cramp up and they would begin to show severe withdrawal symptoms, which no one wanted to deal with. We needed something roughly the same size as these devices to be placed into their hands instead: something that would keep a desired level of interest.

One day at the dollar store, I noticed how sliding puzzles were about the same size as iPods but I saw no true educational value in them, as their tiles arranged to form simple pictures. So, I investigated making ones that had words. Not just words but French verb conjugations! Thus, Tactic*Grams were born: the ultimate French teacher's revenge. They worked like a charm.

AVOIR Tactic*Gram   VOIR Tactic*Gram

That was then. This is now. Today, technology is our friend but keeping up with it is difficult. Popular tech tools and apps get outdated and passed up so quickly. There are tech things that we were using last year that no one even touches this year. I'm talking tech tools that were cool, worked, and were all the rage!

New tech arrives on the market daily. Sometimes we feel like we can't keep up with the pace. Good news! You don't have to be Inspector Gadget by adding every new tech tool to your repertoire. You just have to be aware of what's out there and decide for yourself whether it fits your needs and those of your students.

If you are going to look for new tech tools to tantalize your troupes, consider these points and their subsequent questions:

- **Availability:** Is the tech tool or app easy to access?
- **Affordability:** Is this new tech tool free? How much does it cost? Does it require purchase of specific hardware to operate? Is it within my allowed school budget? Wait! Do I even have a school budget allowance?
- **Viability:** Does this tech tool work within the tech limitations of my school? Do I need internet access to operate it? Can my school internet handle this new tech tool?
- **Accessibility:** Can this new tech tool be used by all of my students? Is this a fair-use product? Does it meet the needs of all my students equally? Does it run on all platforms?
- **Level of need:** Is this tech tool more of a want than a need? Will it promote learning or can the same level of learning be accomplished with strategies that I already have in place?

My advice? Don't abandon the tools that already work for you in favor of the latest new, shiny thing. If you are using magnets on your classroom board, and that works for you and your students, keep it up. If that is the definition of technological advancement that attracts you the most, then perfect!

I know there are many teachers that are cautious about using too much technology in the classroom. I understand their concerns. When it comes to the use of cellphones in the classroom, one of my colleagues told me, "The problem with allowing students to have their cellphones in class is that you're leaving them to their own (electronic) devices."

Technology is more a part of the lives of students than it's ever been. Don't ignore it. If you're looking for the latest tech for your subject area, look no further than your favorite search engine. You will be presented with many new options. Repeat every two months for more options.

Don't wait for tomorrow to try today's technology, because tomorrow may be too late.

JUST BE POSITIVE

ROCKIN' REASON

I know that I can do it, I got the motivation. I know that I can do it, I got determination. I know that I can do it, I got the tools and skills. I know that I can do it, my dreams I will fulfill.

ROCKIN' REQUIREMENTS

- ✓ Positive attitude
- ✓ Pens
- ✓ Paper
- ✓ Desire to make a difference

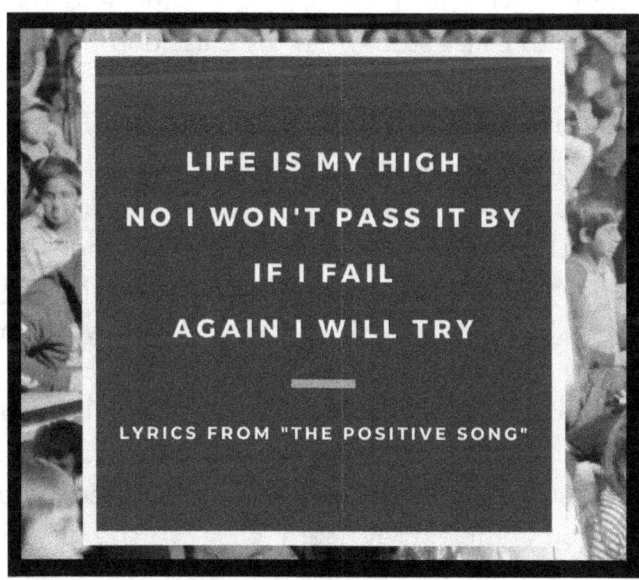

LIFE IS MY HIGH
NO I WON'T PASS IT BY
IF I FAIL
AGAIN I WILL TRY

LYRICS FROM "THE POSITIVE SONG"

My favorite part of a concert is the 20-30 minutes before it begins. I get to go around, meet the concert-goers, and sign a few autographs. This gives the fans a chance to see that I'm just a regular person like them. It's amazing how much I learn in that short period of time. I learn what songs they're hoping to hear, the music styles they like, and I get to gauge how ready they are to sing, dance, and get loud. The time invested before a show helps make a connection; it brings a positive vibe that lasts throughout the entire concert.

In the classroom, the same theory applies. I find that if I take the time to get to know my students, it creates a positive atmosphere that literally carries us throughout the school year. Taking out a few minutes, particularly at the beginning of the school year, to find out how students like to learn, goes a long way to help me gauge how I'll approach implementing teaching and learning strategies that school year.

I really don't think that there's any magic behind this. I think it's the power of feeling acknowledged. Students learn right away that their opinions matter and that I'm ready to listen to them. Because I don't have the time to walk around and have full-on conversations with every student in my classroom, I start the year by handing them out an activity tool called "My Top 3." In this sheet, I ask students to share their interests. The activity tool asks them to list their top three foods, movies, styles of music, hobbies, and sports. It also asks them to fill out a quick survey about learning styles. From this, I will get to see whether they like to learn via reading, writing, or speaking. Finally, the "My Top 3" activity tool asks them to write down three very important numbers: the grade they want to get at the end of the year, the grade they are capable of getting, and the grade that they think they will most likely attain. Grades are very important to students and parents. And now do I not only know their grade goals, I also have information on how they learn best. At the very least, it's a good place to start. The bonus is that for the rest of the year, I have their recorded preferences that I can look back upon. At times when I've seen students struggling in class, I've been able to look back on their responses, meet with them, and help encourage them to better meet their goals.

I take the time to sift through all the information, then I make decisions based on what I read. Some classes prefer reading books, while others prefer film studies. Some classes have a majority preference of writing essays to show knowledge, while others would rather do group work and presentations. I adjust accordingly. Since they're aware that this is the intention of our opening day activity, I'm building a trust with them from the beginning. I'm building a foundation of positivity that will support us throughout the year. This is necessary because things don't always run smoothly throughout an entire semester or year.

Things aren't always rosy in the cabbage patch of pedagogy. Let's switch gears a bit. What should we to do when things are more thorny than rosy? They say that positivity is all in the mind. If you don't mind me asking, how do we stay positive when we're absolutely exhausted from all the marking, planning, organizing, evaluating, and reporting?

Remember that you're a Teacher-Rockstar! Retreat to the one, two, or three songs that pump you up the most. Start your day with those songs. Feel the music. Sing the lyrics. Let them be your mantra to get you through the day. Don't have a song like that? Feel free to borrow this one:

The Positive Song

CHORUS: I know that I can do it, I got the motivation, determination. I know that I can do it, I got the tools and skills. My dreams fulfilled

Here I am. Yo, it's me! DJ E.
From the crib, to the shack, going to sack, rap, attack,
On this well laid-out track
Sing it high, sing it low. Gettin' down good-to-go.
Sit right down and relate, as I lay it out straight
Going to spell out your fate, illustrate, educate
You never know what you're missing, unless you hang around
When they knock you down, get up off the ground
I know where I'm going, I know where I've been
Never cloudin' my brain doin' damage within
Life is my high, no I won't pass it by. If I fail, again I will try. Why?

Can you catch this flow? Tell me what do you know?
I'm so tired of excuses, I'm tired of your lies
Don't tell me you can't do it, you didn't even try
All I hear you do is whine, get out of my crib. Step back, as I adlib
You got all you need, you got what it takes
Don't get lost in the crowd with the phonies and the fakes

Scan the QR code below and watch the lyric video for this song. You may recognize the melody in the chorus.

This is a song I wrote in 2004 to get my students thinking. It's a quick song to encourage them to stay positive, even through the trials and hardships brought on by life.

Here's a complete lesson pack that uses this song as a springboard to discuss matters of positivity. Scan the QR code to download it for free:

Hopefully, the lyrics bring to mind some songs that you love and that positively pump you up. Be sure to choose songs with uplifting lyrics. I laugh when people say, "I don't pay attention to the lyrics; I only listen to the music." You may not be consciously listening to the lyrics, but you're definitely hearing them. So, choose your songs wisely. Then, if you don't have one already, create a playlist of positive songs.

Whether I'm exhausted from teaching or I'm reflecting upon life in the hotel room between concerts, there are times when I need a positive tune to lift me up. From my experience, my emotional and mental health greatly improve when I'm enjoying a positive tune. I can't get enough of them. What's your favorite song to fire you up when you're feeling watered down? Put down this book and start your playlist with the first song that came to your mind.

Let's get back to business. Let's discuss ways that we can involve our students in spreading positivity in the classroom and throughout the school. Here is a list of just a few:

- Have your students write positive messages on sticky notes and have them stick them on lockers, walls, and binders.
- Keep track of students' birthdays (even those that are outside of school days). You don't to need sing Happy Birthday or bake a cake. A quick, small acknowledgment will suffice.

- Make mental notes of students' interests. If students are involved with house league or travel sports, chances are they played games on the weekend. Ask them how their games went. Set the example and you will see students do the same.
- Create a positive song playlist for each class to play while students are doing seatwork. Pre-listen to all songs, of course.
- Work with your class to create, plan, and execute random acts of kindness across the school and/or local community.
- Have students create small "Thank You" notes to put in teacher mailboxes. Don't forget your administration, custodians, administrative assistants, bus drivers, cafeteria workers, etc.
- Discuss with your class the attributes of a superhero. What makes a hero? How can we be heroes?
- At random times, pick one student and tell them that you're proud of them. Be sure to take the time to explain why.
- Make good news communication reports to parents. These help build a positive, trilateral relationship between teacher, parents/guardians and student.
- Invite your administration to view students' work or invite them to special events happening in your classroom.
- Display student work and have students participate in gallery walks, leaving a positive comment about the work of others.
- Encourage students, colleagues, and administration to attend school team events that you coach.
- Make a run to the dollar store and purchase little items related to your course of study to decorate your classroom. Buy some stickers. Students of all ages love stickers!
- Add students' names to activity tools, quizzes, tests, and exams.
- Recognize students with certificates.
- Have a library of positive literature that students can read when done work or even sign out and take home.
- At the end of a semester or school year, have students record a positive video message for next year's group. Graduates can do the same for newcomers.

- Work together with your class to create short, positive messages to be read during morning announcements.
- Take ten minutes out of your class time and do a school yard clean-up.
- Celebrate the personal triumphs of your students: piano recitals, sports games, competitions, spelling bees, etc.
- Involve the local media in celebrating any significant moments of positivity that you're spreading that are making a difference in your school or community.
- Have your students write positive letters or emails to members of your government. They can be communications of encouragement or those offering ideas for positive change.

The possibilities for spreading positivity are numerous. Spreading positivity is contagious. Please note that some ideas will work better than others depending on your class situation. Let me share with you one idea that absolutely came crashing down on me.

I tried an experiment once in my class: I thought I'd use science to create a positive situation. I had two students that were both behaving negatively and being disruptive in class. They were seated far from each other, on opposite sides of the classroom. Two negatives equal a positive, right? So, I did the scientifically logical thing: I sat them right next to each other so that the negative behaviors would cancel each other out. Let me tell you, these two seated together did not equal a positive outcome. I concluded that I'm not very good at science.

Positivity is the best policy no matter what. Even when the going gets tough, the tough get positive. It's an action as much as it's a state of being.

KEEP UP

ROCKIN' REASON

Trends come and go, but riding a current trend can keep things fresh in the classroom and create connections and lasting memories.

ROCKIN' REQUIREMENTS

- ✓ Internet
- ✓ Creator platforms
- ✓ Electronic devices
- ✓ Social media
- ✓ Streaming or subscription services
- ✓ Willingness to keep up on trends

GLOSSARY OF TEACHER-ROCKSTAR PARALLELS

YEARS TAUGHT = TOUR EXPERIENCE

EXPERIENCED TEACHERS HAVE ROCKED THE ROAD LESS TRAVELLED. ASK THEM FOR ADVICE. THEY ARE YOUR PROFESSIONAL GPS.

In 1994, the song "Basket Case" was a huge hit by an upstart band named Green Day. The fall of that same year, I decided to borrow the melody to the chorus of that song to syllabically replace their words with some French, fast-food vocabulary that I wanted my students to learn (see tip "That's A Rap" for more details on this method). It worked to perfection. Soon, my students were singing:

Sur mon hamburger garçon: du ketchup et des cornichons,
(Sometimes I give myself the creeps, Sometimes my mind plays tricks on me.)
du relish, des oignons, de la mayo, du bacon,
(It all keeps adding up.   I think I'm cracking up.)
de la moutarde, de la laitue, et du fromage
(Am I just paranoid?   Or am I just stoned?)

They learned the vocabulary and even learned their partitive articles. Partitive articles aren't always the easiest to teach.

All was well until my students started going to the Stratford Cullitons hockey games. The Cullitons are the town's Jr. B hockey team. In between periods, popular songs would play over the PA system to keep the crowd entertained. Each time the song "Basket Case" was played, about 100 teenagers would burst out singing the French, fast-food version of the song: right there in public. Visitors, parents, grandparents, and the like would turn around and look at the group of teens and openly wonder, "Who is their cult leader?!" In this case, that was me. Oops.

You can lead students to knowledge, but you can't make them think. You need to think of ways to lead them to that knowledge. Keeping up with trends is one way to do that. Keeping up with trends allows you to blend their cultural interests with your devious plans to cover the curriculum of your subject area.

I've composed educational songs in all different types of musical genres: rock, rap, grunge, heavy metal, electronic dance, blues, reggae, and pop. It keeps me fresh as a creator, but more importantly, it provides fresh content and new learning opportunities for students. This variety also ensures that I'm appealing to the different musical tastes of my students.

I've had to learn to adapt with new styles of music that have come along. When electronic-based music became more mainstream, I began to compose music that was very different than anything I had ever done before. So different, in fact, that I had to release that new music under a different stage-name, DJ DELF. I learned that the key is to stay constantly open to changes in trends. When trap music, or "mumble rap" as it's sometimes referred to, became popular, I released an Étienne song called ÊTRE II in that style. I share all of this simply to show that by being open, I have been able to continue to reach students as an international touring artist. Keeping up with trends has allowed me to reinvent myself and my outlook on my professional life. In the classroom, keeping up with trends has allowed me to do the same.

Let me list for you some trends that I have used to help make learning more engaging for my students. My hope is that it'll inspire you to come up with some on your own. I will omit the year in these examples so that you can have some fun guessing the era from which these trends came.

- When backwards was the only way to wear your baseball hat, I sometimes flipped mine around and rapped a quick rap lesson for my students.
- When the Olympics come around, I often break my classes into teams and run mini-learning competitions (medals included).

- When retro videos games were back in style, I actually tried my hand at being a video game creator. I created two French learning-games based off of the popular 1980s video games Frogger and Pac-Man. The two years that these video games were available online, many students enjoyed trying to earn the high score while learning some French along the way.

- The sudden rise in popularity of social media platforms that use short video clips to entertain, spurred me to challenge students to make small presentation videos or study videos for upcoming tests.
- When Facebook became commonplace across social media, I created various learning tasks for students, including having them create their own "Fakebook" profile in French.
- I will even combine two trends. I combined the popularity of Fortnite (video game) dancing with the "Baby Shark" song, in order to teach my students proper use of French accents.

- When the trend of planking became popular, I challenged my students to snap quick photos of themselves or their classmates planking in order to teach a long list of French prepositions.

- When the TV show CSI was all my students could talk about, I went into our school yard and buried items related to an upcoming History unit. They had to dig, investigate, and record their findings. This was a great springboard to start the unit.
- When all my students were obsessed with the Macarena dance, I allowed them to dance it during the verses when we learned the song ALLER.
- The Ice Bucket Challenge was something that we couldn't do in class, but it did inspire my idea of hosting a cross-class video challenge. Since I taught many classes, I had a class create a challenge related to our subject area. They filmed themselves doing the challenge and then sent the challenge to another class. That class had to complete the challenge and create one of their own in the spirit of one-upping each other.

Some trends stick around longer than others. I still get messages across social media from fans that find me on TikTok. Unwillingly, I became TikTok "famous" when a 20-year-old TikTok "celebrity" posted a video with him dancing to my song ALLER. It went viral. My socials blew up about this and many people asked me to join TikTok and do a reply video. I conceded. That reply video then became viral, and my TikTok account (@rockyourclass) became Tik Tok "famous." Again, I just rode the trend.

How do we stay up-to-date with current trends? Ask your students. If you don't want to do so directly, you can hand out an "interests" sheet for you to collect and keep for later reference, or you can do an online search for "current popular trends." Most will not apply, but some might be the perfect recipe to blend trends with curriculum ends.

LET ME SPELL IT OUT

ROCKIN' REASON

No matter what subject area you teach, there is one common issue that all teachers notice: our students' ability to spell properly is on the D-E-C-L-I-N-E.

ROCKIN' REQUIREMENTS

- ✓ Computers
- ✓ Course content
- ✓ Pen
- ✓ Paper
- ✓ A list of your unit study's keywords

I've had the privilege of touring with musician Roland Bibeau as my guitarist for many years. We've travelled all over Canada and the United States together. As a result, we have many road-warrior stories. One in particular that sticks with me is the time that we were on the road heading to a show in London, Ontario, Canada. One thing you have to know about Roland is that he is a no-nonsense guy; a straight shooter. He doesn't like it when you beat around the bush. He prefers you to simply spell it out, whether good or bad. Another thing about Roland is that he also doesn't like changes in routine or surprises. This is why I made it a particular point to inform him in advance, on our way to London, that this particular show was going to have special guests seated in the front rows. Here's exactly how the conversation went:

"Roland?" I started. "I have to tell about the one school that is coming to our show today."

"Okay, what about them?" he replied while his eyes focused on the task of driving us down the highway.

"The first two rows will be filled with students from a school for the blind," I explained. "We're seating them there so that they can be closer to us, but I'm telling you this because they may not react the same as other students that we've had in the front rows at other shows. They may not be able to pick up on all our visual cues."

"Uh huh," replied Roland. "Got it."

I could see that as he was driving, he was processing everything that I had just told him. Not two minutes later, he nearly slammed on the brakes in the middle of highway as he turned to me with a flustered look on his face and said, "Wait! If they're from a school for the blind, how are they gonna hear us?!"

I just smiled, shook my head and said, "Roland. They're blind. They're not deaf."

"Oh, oh. Right!" he exclaimed as he resumed normal driving speeds, yet continued to try and sort it all out in his head. In his defence, he hadn't had his morning coffee yet.

I think that a lot of teachers are like Roland. Yes, we need our coffee, but more than that, we are straight shooters. We don't like change, and we like things spelled out. Give us the truth. Well, the truth is that when it comes to our students spelling words out, things have changed — and not for the better.

No matter what subject area you teach, teachers in staff rooms across the globe share one common complaint: the decline of students' ability to spell correctly. You may be surprised to learn that it's even an acute problem for your Math colleagues who are disappointed (to put it mildly) in the spelling that they see from students in math word problems.

Let me shoot straight here: I don't want to hear the excuses. It's not the time to blame it on the fact that students are no longer taught cursive handwriting. It's not the time to blame spell-check apps and autocorrecting software, either. Complaining won't change a thing. Complaining about spelling is like trying to do sign language wearing oven mitts: it's a complete waste of time.

The cure? Let's band together across all subject areas and stress the importance of spelling with our students. It's in this discipline that students will develop an attention to detail that will increase the understanding of even those harder-to-learn concepts in your subject area. Before we tackle hard-to-spell words in your subject area, let's begin by tackling the most commonly misspelled words in the English language. Let's work together so that <u>there</u> ability to spell is <u>their</u> when they need <u>they're</u> spelling! Cue the music.

Mispeled Wirdz

This isn't a song, **though** it goes on and on,
With a strong beat, there's no **deceit**,
In my words, so don't **retreat**
Let me **separate** you from **misspelled** words you'll meet
This **feat** of proper spelling you can complete
By the **hour** you'll sit **here** and **hear** our speech
We'll form a **committee** and keep proper spelling within reach
Whether today or **tomorrow** or a **Wednesday** in **February**
Don't you know that learning how to spell is **necessary**?
You've heard the catch phrases from infancy
Like "i" before "e" **except** after "c"
But the English language has **exceptions** that **exceed**
Let me proceed so you'll **succeed**; **success** is **guaranteed**
Be **courageous**, there's an "e" in **changeable**
But drop the "e" if your **argument** is not **valuable**
They're not to **desert** their **dessert** in the **desert** over there
Or wave their hands in frustration in the **air** when they **err**
I'm **already** ready. Are you **all ready** to go?
It's time to **know which witch** said "**No!**"
Or why only **half** the horses **have heard**
The **hoarse** cow singing from the **herd**
Never wait or be late for a **scheduled practice**
Accept the fact that you need to **practise**
Receive, **believe** this **message** I **write**
As I **massage** these words and make spelling **right**
For example "i.e." it was a great **relief**,
That the **chief** ran into **field** and caught the **thief**
His sheer **height** and **weight** meant he **seized** him without **grief**
Let me **wrap** up this **rap**. Take the **advice** that I **advise** and **recognize**

When it comes to words that sound the same
There are more than **two**, in fact **too** many for me **to** name
And if you think it's **impossible**, try to get **capable**
Because words with tricky endings are **plentiful**
Don't feel **dumb** if the **bomb** of silent letters comes your way
Just **whistle** this **hymn** (in your head) until you get it **straight**
Don't be **stopped** by double letters making **misspelled** words
There is really no secret you'll have to practice until it works
Remember this **ridiculous** spellbound rhythm 'cause it is **through**
I thought that you **knew**.
No? There's nothing **new** to know
Believe me this song has effect,
Except if you don't **accept** it, you won't be **affected**

The song Mispeled Wirdz hosts almost 100 of the most commonly misspelled words in the English language. You can scan the QR codes to access the music video to the song and get a free download of the Mispeled Wirdz Activity Package, as well.

Scan this QR code to access the music video for the song Mispeled Wirdz

Scan this QR code to download a free copy of the Mispeled Wirdz Package

It's true that we have more on our plates than just a need for better spelling; we have curriculum to cover — but wait! What if we included spelling as part of that curriculum coverage?

Here are a list of some spelling-related activities that you can add to your list of learning strategies when engaging students in keywords of any unit study:

- **Word Jumbles:** Create an activity tool where students have to unscramble the letters to keywords from your unit study.
- **Scrabble™:** Allow your students to play games of Scrabble where the use of keywords from your subject area or unit of study are worth three times the points.
- **Spelling Bee:** Host a spelling bee in your class before a unit test. After the word is spelled correctly, use the opportunity to discuss the keyword in more depth.
- **Wheel of Fortune™:** Have a ready-made list of keywords that you want your students to spell. Have students take turns throwing a single die. If they roll 1-4, that is the amount of consonant letters they get to guess. If they roll a 5, they get to guess a vowel. If they roll a 6, they can unveil any hidden letter.
- **Hangman:** Divide the class into two teams. Students guess a mystery keyword letter by letter. If the letter they guess is a part of the mystery word, that letter is revealed. If not, then part of a picture is drawn. If the picture is drawn before the word is revealed, the guessing team loses. This traditional game has become much more politically correct now. Please do not draw a hanged man. Instead, draw any figure that can be assembled in ten lines.

Tiptoeing around the issue of improper spelling is like trying to drown a fish: the idea is cruel and helps no one. It's pointless. When you do take the time to include spelling while covering a unit study, you are not only benefitting the students at the present moment, you are creating building blocks for future teachers that your students will encounter. Do it for the students. Do it for the team. Do it for Roland!

MIME TIME

ROCKIN' REASON

Sometimes you say more by saying nothing at all.

ROCKIN' REQUIREMENTS

✓ Visual aids   ✓ Audio aids

✓ Tactile aids   ✓ Smelling aids

✓ Course content ✓ Tape (optional)

I was nearing the end of three months straight of concerts when it happened: I was ready to start a show, the music began playing, I brought the microphone to my mouth, but no sound escaped my lips. I had lost my voice. Fortunately, just as our students can surprise us in class, the thousands of students at the concert stepped up big time. There was nothing I could do. I pointed the mic out towards the audience and they began singing the song for me. They continued singing for the rest of the concert, track after track.

A few years later, a similar experience happened, this time in the classroom. I started to teach a class when my voice gave out. This time, I had no mic to point towards my students. Even if I did, would they know what to do or say? I was in the middle of a new lesson. What was I to do? I snapped into Mime Time mode: I pointed to objects, I used gestures, I wrote keywords on the board, and I did anything that would get my point across. These techniques turned out to be silent but deadly accurate. I challenged myself and my students to see just how long I could keep the lesson going. I did it. I finished the ten minute lesson and handed out the follow-up activity work. I had stumbled onto another cool strategy.

My students, whether out of sympathy or out of the sheer challenge, tried to interpret for me as I taught the lesson. They stepped up and they delivered. I decided that I wouldn't wait until my voice gave out again. I decided that I was going to plan another Mime Time lesson. I created a template that included my lesson title, goals, keywords, and phrases. Then, I filled an inventory checklist of objects and props that I thought might work. Before the lesson began, I wrote the keywords and phrases randomly on the board. I placed various objects and props around the classroom. I even put some on the desks of specific students. During the lesson, when I pointed to those students, they held up the objects and the remaining students tried to figure out the connection.

That's it. That's the Mime Time strategy. Need I say more? Give it a go. Deliver a five to ten minute lesson without saying a word. The break in routine alone will have your students' full attention, and the forced use of their other senses will make this lesson unforgettable.

I'm sharing with you the Mime Time template that I use for this strategy. Try it, edit it, share it. Grab the free download of the Mime Time lesson plan pack by scanning the QR code above.

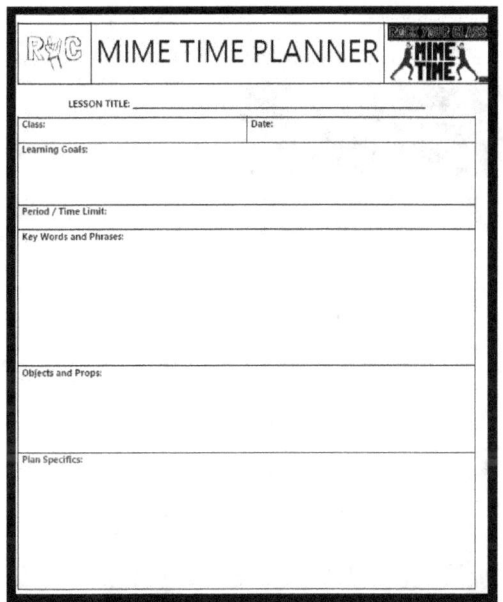

They say silence is golden. Maybe this will be a golden idea for you to try with your students. Best part? You don't have to dress up like a mime; they're scary. I was once yelled at by a mime in Paris. It hurt, but then I wondered if it really happened; however I know that it did because I understand French.

One might think that the idea of not talking to our students while delivering a lesson is about as smart as reading in the dark. On the contrary, this is an enlightened idea. Give your students the silent treatment my fellow Teacher-Rockstars!

NEEDS MORE ART

ROCKIN' REASON

Speaking, listening, reading, and writing should not be the only ways that we evaluate our students. Visual arts can be another way that students show knowledge.

ROCKIN' REQUIREMENTS

- ✓ Computers
- ✓ Paper
- ✓ Color paper
- ✓ Course content
- ✓ Colored pencils or markers
- ✓ Art supplies

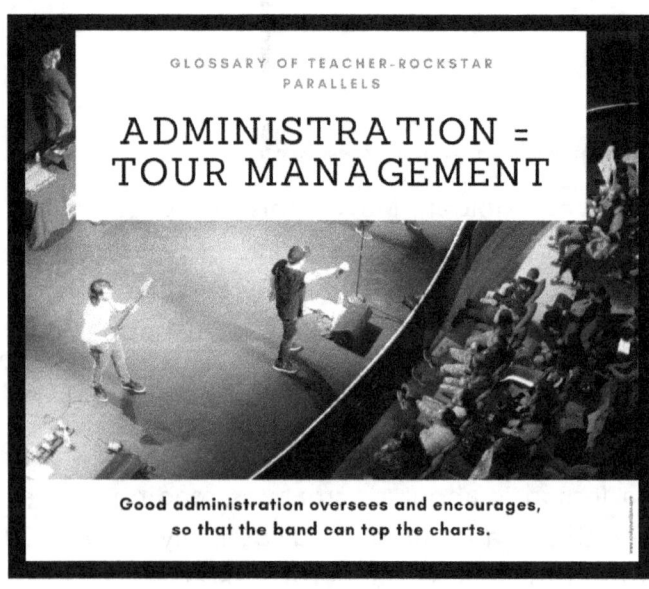

It can be very frustrating when you're writing a song and you suddenly become stuck. Maybe you're missing a good idea for a verse, a chorus, or a melody? It's hard writing a good song.

It's like making dinner. Have you ever tried to make dinner and felt that it was missing a little something-something? Maybe it needs more salt? Needs some spice? As a teacher, have you ever made a lesson plan and felt that it was just missing something? A catch, a hook, or a grabber? Whatever it is, you have the feeling that things just aren't right. Well, that is education without the arts. I mean, DAM! No, not damn. I mean, DAM. Drama, arts (visual), and music. Shout out to the arts!

Since some of the other A-Z tips in this book cover drama and music, let's focus on visual arts for this tip. Art is everywhere. Art is eternal. It's based in the he*art*, at the core of p*art*icipation, and at the end of every st*art*. It's the "A" that you see at STEAM teacher conferences (Science, Tech, Engineering, Arts, Math).

Ever doodle when you're bored? Ever see students doodling or drawing before, during, or after lessons? These are the type of people that would excel at showing curriculum content knowledge through visual arts. The rest of us that can't draw? We could be well-served to give it a go and put to work connections in our brain that may be otherwise underutilized.

Here are ten visual arts challenges that I've offered my students as a way to show curriculum content knowledge:

1. **Draw me this.** Provide sentences or challenges and have students draw in boxes to show knowledge. You may wish to ask them to draw and label.

2. **The Michelangelo Method.** Have students engage in a curriculum-related activity where they have to draw or work from underneath their desks. Have them use magnets or tape to hold the paper up underneath their desks. Post your students' finished work on ceilings (if permitted by your administration).

3. **Win, Lose, or Draw.** Using terms from the current unit that you're studying, make a list of vocabulary words that can be drawn. Have students play a classic game of win, lose, or draw. Pause during the game to use their drawings as teachable moments to expand on ideas and concepts.

4. **Gallery Walks.** Have students draw full posters covering several elements of a unit study. Number and display the finished posters around the class. Have students present and explain their works of art, or have the class circulate and record observations on at least five of the works of art. What do they see? What do they learn from studying this gallery work of art?

5. **Back-to-Back.** In pairs, have students sit back-to-back with one another. One student describes while the other one draws. The description can be from a pre-made script or spontaneous but related to your current curriculum study. When a description is done, have the students face each other and analyze the completed drawing. Does it match the description?

6. **Etch A Sketch™.** Pick up some Etch A Sketch™ devices from the dollar store or a thrift store. Have students make curriculum content-related drawings. Share. Discuss. Erase. Repeat.

7. **Carbon Paper.** An affordable art activity that can be done with carbon paper. Place a carbon paper between two blank pieces of paper. On the top blank sheet, have students trace out

a design with their fingernail or a blunt object (without leaving a viewable image on the top sheet). After they're done, remove the top blank paper and the carbon paper to reveal the final product that was produced from the drawing transposed from the top to the last sheet via the carbon paper. Share. Discuss. Repeat with new bottom paper.

8. **Lego™.** Pick up some old Legos from a thrift shop or from yard sales. Have students work in groups to create scenes related to your current unit of study. Upon completion, have students give a tour of their construction to show knowledge.

9. **Finger Painting.** Just as students of all ages love stickers, most would jump at the chance to finger paint. Challenge your students to make visual art pieces via finger painting that vibrantly depict concepts they're learning.

10. **Playing with Playdough.** You can make homemade playdough or pick some up at the dollar store. Challenge your students to make statues and monuments out of playdough. Then, ask them to write a thorough description of the piece.

Put plainly, my Teacher-Rockstar friends: a picture is worth a thousand concepts learned!

OUT THE DOOR

ROCKIN' REASON

The grass isn't always greener in the classroom. Escape the four walls of the classroom, and allow your students to experience new learning environments.

ROCKIN' REQUIREMENTS

- ✓ Shovel
- ✓ Curriculum content
- ✓ Gymnasium
- ✓ Support from administration
- ✓ Support from custodian
- ✓ Props

I'll always give credit where credit is due. The reason why I'm able to perform sold-out shows in front of thousands of students in theaters and arenas is because of the teachers. They're the ones that book the tickets and leave the schools (sometimes early in the morning) in packed busses to make their way to the shows. Furthermore, I think it's no secret that a big part of the reason why students love going to an Étienne concert, and why they're all such loud and crazy fans, is because they get to get out of school! For that moment in time, I'm a hero of sorts because the concert is a great excuse for them to escape the four walls of the classroom.

Sometimes, change is good. Changing the learning environment for students can be a part of that. Change brings people out of their comfort zone. Sometimes, we have to teach outside of our comfort zone. Sometimes by choice, sometimes by force.

Some of my most successful lessons have taken place outside the four walls of the classroom, and I will credit my students' excitement for being a big part of the success of those lessons.

My degree is in French Language and Literature, but I've taught Math, Guidance, Computers, English, and History. History came as a surprise. One day, I was suddenly assigned a grade 7 History class. What did I know about History? To me, history was all in the past! I had never taught History. So, I channeled my former student-self. How would I want to learn history if I was a student? Certainly not by copying notes all year long. Certainly not by focusing only on the memorization of dates and events. I wanted my students to dig deep into history. So, that's what we did! I organized a "real" archeological dig for my students. What better way for them to uncover true learning?

With permission from my administration and the custodial staff, I found a plot of land on school property and gently buried objects that were related to the curriculum content. I taught my students a basic lesson on how to conduct an archeological dig. I divided the class into teams and assigned roles of diggers, cleaners, labellers, transporters, artists, and investigators. My students set off on the task of doing an excavation for information. They unearthed the gems that I had hidden. They brought those items back to the classroom, cleaned them off, drew them, recorded them, and studied them closely. Together as a class, they put the pieces together and tried to tell the story of what had transpired years back over that plot of land. It served as a great springboard for learning, and I believe it was a history lesson they'll never forget.

Interestingly enough, my students found objects that I did not bury, including pieces of clay pottery, fragments of fine china plates, coins, and coal fragments. Those additional findings spurred me to do some research. I learned that before our school was erected, there was a steel factory on the property that manufactured weaponry during the Second World War.

If you're not ready to grab a shovel and dig in the school yard, no problem. Here's a list of some other places where you can escape the four walls of the classroom and unearth some cool learning moments. I'll leave the creative ideas of what to do in these locales up to you and your students:

- Reserve access to the school gymnasium.
- Spend time in the large, open spaces of a school playground.
- Find access to a nearby park.
- Book space at a school or local theater.
- Access your school drama room (if applicable).

- Gain access to a school culinary classroom or kitchen.
- Swap your classroom with the science teacher and spend some time in the school science lab.
- Get your art on and swap classes with your school art teacher (if applicable).
- Make some music in the school music room (if applicable).
- Book a field trip. Even an Étienne concert can serve as a glorified field trip.
- Visit a local heritage museum.
- Record some raps with students at a local recording studio.
- Explore your town or city government building(s).
- Allow your students to experience your current unit of study via food. Call a local restaurant and arrange a sit-down meal.
- Book it over to the local library.
- Get physical at your local sportsplex.
- Take a walk through town and study local street names.

Okay, I know that I told you to come up with your own ideas, but I can't resist. Prepare a game of Amazing Race™ for your students that will see them making their way all over the school. Create challenging clues that force students to think. For example, rather than just telling them to head to the library after they solve clue #1, have the next instruction read, "Now, visit the school's keeper of the books to pick up clue #2." Instead of writing, "Head to the east side of the sports field," have the end of clue #2 read, "Visit the side of the school sports field where the sun rises, to collect clue #3." Have fun with it! Each clue should include a challenge that students have to solve related to your current unit of study in order for them to move on to the next clue.

They say that the grass is always greener on the other side. Well, the grass is most likely outside. Escape those four walls with your students, my fellow Teacher-Rockstars!

PLAY WITH MATCHES

ROCKIN' REASON

To provide playful, pedagogical pair practice with curriculum content while moving, matching, and having fun. Meaningful matching to make memorizing memorable.

ROCKIN' REQUIREMENTS

- ✓ Paper
- ✓ Scissors
- ✓ Microsoft Word or equivalent

A key factor to putting on a good concert is the visual element of the show. I like to have videos playing behind me on a huge screen. I love to perform under a lot of bright, moving lights. That's why I always wear sunglasses on stage; the lights are so bright that I often cannot see anyone in the audience, save for the fans in the first two rows. Lasers lights and smoke or fog machines don't hurt either. The more effects, the better. The one thing I've never had at my show is pyrotechnics. It's not that I don't like to play with fire. Not at all. It's just that pyrotechnics require a special permit and a licenced operator at the show. Believe me, if I could have it, there would be fire at my shows. Since I can't, I bring the fire to my classroom when I let my students play with matches.

Judge me as you will but, yes, I let my students play with matches. Oh, I know. If you play with fire, you'll get burned, but if you play with matches, your lessons will be on fire. Things get heated up in my class as my students get on fire for match play. The question isn't why I'm letting my students play with matches. The question is: are you doing the same?

Matching plays to the most basic, fundamental understanding that humans cling to: logic. Things have to make sense in the mind. The mind finds peace in logic and reason. The mind smiles when things fit together: salt and pepper, peanut butter and jelly, pencil and paper, hammer and nail, or a burger and fries. All of these are almost automatic word associations. Like water to thirst, humans feel quenched when everything is matched and everything is in its right place; the universe rejoices.

As a teacher, I play on my students' need to see everything fit, make sense, and match in their minds. So, I let them play with matches. One of my favorite activities to do with matching is something my colleague, Maddy Shipton, calls "Méli-Mélo" in French. This works for all grades and subject areas.

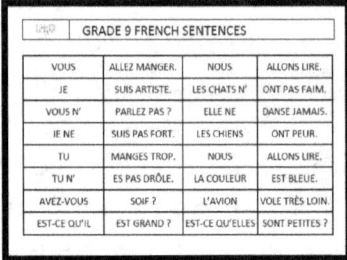

First, complete a grid with 16 problems and 16 corresponding solutions, or you can fill the grid with matching sentence fragments, terms, definitions, or anything that can be paired. For this lesson, we'll go with 32 as an average class size. You can adjust according to your class size. After you've filled out the grid, cut out the 32 game pieces. Distribute one per student. How you distribute the pieces is up to you: you can stand at the door as students file in and hand one to each student, you can place one face down on each of the students' desks, or you can have them

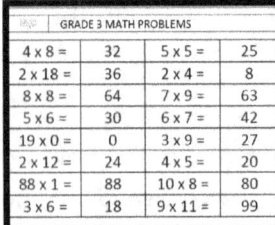
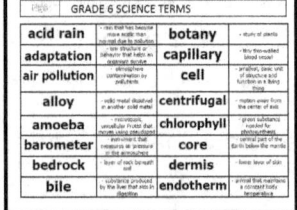

come up to you and pick from a pile. Once every student has a game piece, start a song. If you have a song that's related to the content of the matching activity, great. If not, I recommend an upbeat, instrumental track. Play the song for one minute while students circulate, looking for their match. When they find their match, they can either sit down together or go to a designated area in the classroom that you've pre-determined. Stop the music after one minute and see how many pairs the class was able to make. Have students read their matched pieces aloud to the rest of the class. You can collect and redistribute the pieces to play again.

Here's a cool alternative: use the 32 pieces as a puzzle to be solved by one student at their desk. Time each student as they do this individual re-pairing challenge. This is perfect for any homeschool or school situation. Ready to try it? I went ahead and did the grunt work for you. Download your free complete lesson

 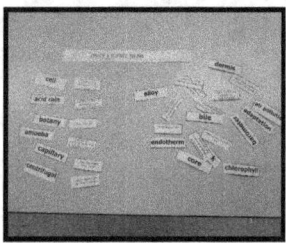 

plan package by scanning the QR code below. Your blank grid is ready for you to complete. In case you need it, scan the other QR code to gain access to a high-energy, instrumental track for your students as they repair their content knowledge with this re-pairing, matching activity.

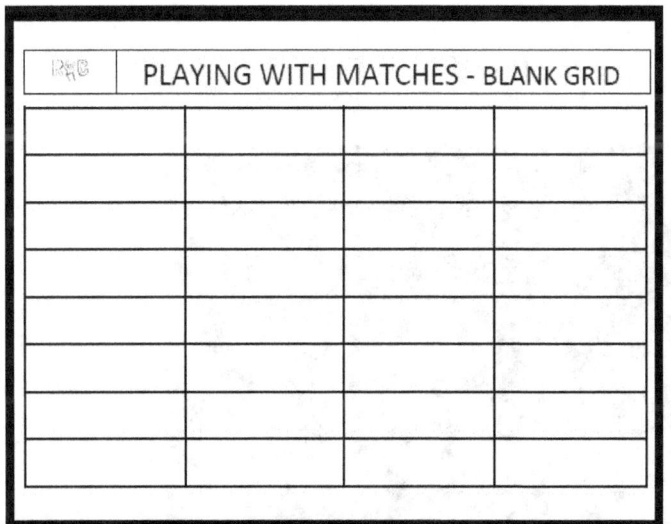

Scan this QR code to download the Playing With Matches Package

Scan this QR code for access to a high-energy instrumental song

It's even apparent to parents that pairs are meant to be a perfect match between curriculum taught and curriculum understood. Give it a go, my Teacher-Rockstar friends!

QUESTION EVERYTHING

ROCKIN' REASON

What better way to get answers than by asking questions? How far can questions take us on the path of learning? How many questions does it take to spark our students' learning lightbulbs?

ROCKIN' REQUIREMENTS

- ✓ Computer
- ✓ Course content
- ✓ Pen and Paper
- ✓ Printer
- ✓ Questions
- ✓ More questions

One speaker. No speakers. When you book a concert tour, you never know what to expect. To put on a proper concert, you need at least two speakers. Stereo. Otherwise, you're just going to give the audience mono. Sorry, old musician's joke. I've had a few performances with only one working speaker. The tough part is remembering to pay attention to both sides of the crowd, even if only one side is getting all the sound. It's kind of like teaching to one side of the class while risking the possibility of losing the attention of the other side.

One time while touring in New Zealand, I had a show in Auckland. When I arrived, I learned that the equipment was fried: nothing worked. 400 students packed in a tiny theater and no working sound equipment. Fifteen minutes before showtime, the teachers were nervous, but not me. I love a challenge. I had learned long ago that there's always an answer. The key is to ask the right questions. I asked the people in charge of the theater if they had a "boombox." For those of a younger generation, a boombox is a plug-in, portable, music playing device with built-in speakers. Fortunately, they had one. We popped nine batteries into it, I placed a background music CD in the boombox, and I spent the entire hour-long show moving around the crowd singing out loud (no microphone) to the music blasting from it.

The students were incredible. They were singing, dancing, wearing their Étienne temporary tattoos, and waving their homemade signs during the entire show. Problems arise from time to time, but there's always a solution. The key is to keep asking questions.

Just as the squeaky wheel gets the oil, the questioner gets the answers. Good things may come to those who wait, but better things come to those who interrogate. Do you believe in the power of asking questions? Are questions not where answers come from? Did you know that I repeat this mantra often to my students and to my own children? How can you get answers if you don't ask questions?

A question word poem:
>I have some questions that I must raise,
>Ask, pose, and rephrase.
>They're designed to get you out of a haze
>And bring you to answers that will amaze.
>Who, what, why, when, where, how;
>Come on and ask them now.
>I wanna hear it loud,
>Who? What? Why? When? Where? How?

One day, I decided to put the power of questions to the test. I had witnessed the success of the Question Game in our drama club at Juliet Public School in Stratford, Ontario. My colleague, Lynn MacDonald, and I used to have our students play it. In the Question Game, students form two lines, with the lead persons of each line facing one another. The students begin a conversation using only questions. If a student responds to their opponent's question with a statement, they're eliminated. The person behind them (on their team) takes their place. When the last student is eliminated, the team that's still standing wins.

This is unquestionably a great drama activity, and there's no question that this game inspired me to try it as a teaching strategy. I decided to teach a five to ten minute lesson using only question words. Do you think it worked? Was my mission accomplished? You got this far into the book, and you dare question yet another crazy tip? Could I manage to write the rest of this entire chapter using only question words? Probably. Oops. I'm eliminated. Your turn.

Back to the lesson. Here's how I did it: I was going to teach a small unit from the grade 7 History textbook, and I read through the chapter in advance. I looked at the chapter questions that I would be assigning after my lesson and studied all the answers to those questions. I grabbed a pen and paper and weaved everything into my question lesson plan. Or, is it a questionable lesson plan? You decide. In three columns, I isolated all the facts, historical figures, and dates that I wanted my students to learn. Finally, I created a question formula page so that I could plug in the facts, figures, and dates into the templated questions and create a quick lesson conversation. I did this so that I would have a list of possible templated questions to use with future lessons. Just plug in and go.

Here are just some templated questions that I created:
- Did you know that (fact #1)?
- Who, other than (key historical figure #1), would come up with (fact #2)?
- If you were presented with (fact #3), would that not make sense?
- What better time in history than (date #1) to have (fact #4) take place?
- How many historical figures played a part in (fact #5), you ask?
- Would you believe (key historical figures #2, #3, and #4) all had their hand in (fact #5)?
- Without (fact #5), how would (fact #6) happen?
- In what year did (fact #6) take place? Would you believe (date #2)?
- That was 10 years before (date #3), wasn't it?
- And what happened in (date #3), you're wondering? Don't you think I'll tell you?
- Isn't it interesting to learn that (fact #7) happened in (date #3)?

When I tried this with my students, they were completely engaged. Until I pointed it out, some students didn't even realize that I had taught the entire lesson posing only questions. My advice? If you try this tip with your students, please finish your lesson with this final question: any questions?

ROUTINES ROOT TEENS

ROCKIN' REASON

Students are coming to you from other classes. How can we have them focusing in on your course content from the first minute of class right until the bell rings? Routines root teens.

ROCKIN' REQUIREMENTS

✓ Screen

✓ Pen

✓ Paper

✓ Curriculum content

✓ Electronic devices

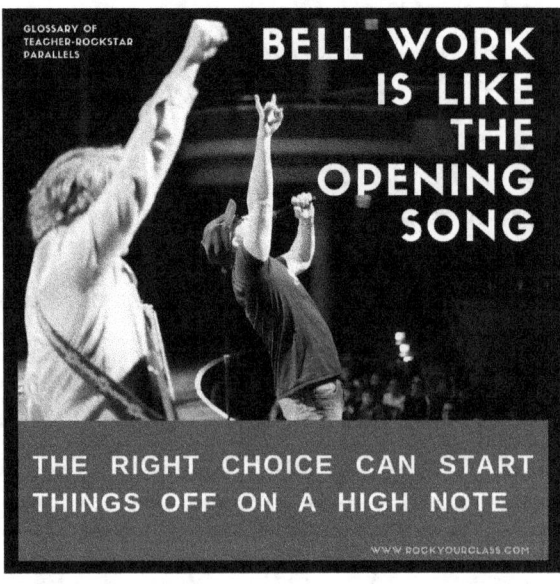

Choosing the right song to start off a concert is very important. That opening tune sets the tone for the rest of the show. You don't want to start off with a super slow song and bore the audience, and you don't want to give them your best stuff first (the stuff they came to hear). Where would you go from there? The opener has to be full of energy. It has to engage the audience, get them interested, and get them anticipating the excitement ahead. No matter what was on their minds before they sat in their seats, you want to make them forget everything and join you on this musical journey that you've planned.

Same goes for the classroom. Like the early bird that catches the worm, the earlier you grab student interest, the better. When you begin your lesson at the beginning of a period, students will have just transitioned from another subject area. You must cleanse their minds of the content of the previous subject and properly prepare them to set their sights on this subject area. But how?

Much like a lesson plan, my concerts are designed to start with a bang. The first three songs are designed to get students screaming and singing along. This sets the tone for the rest of the concert. The show then moves to the middle or meatier part of the performance, featuring a few songs that make fans think. The concert ends with non-stop action and songs that get students up and moving. These last songs are the ones that will still be playing in their heads the rest of the day.

This is not unlike my classroom formula. I begin the first part of my class doing dynamic Bell Work. Bell Work is a popular term for a warm-up or opening class activity. It's the first task that you ask students to complete as they come into class. It's an activity designed to cleanse them of lingering thoughts from the class before, so they can concentrate on a more important subject area: the one you are about to teach!

As a French teacher, I decided to create my own Bell Work activities called the DJ DELF Dailies. The Dailies are my go-to because they include pre-made animated videos that take students through their Bell Work. They come with all the student activity recording tools and the teacher assessment and evaluation grids already prepared. I want to highlight what I consider to be the best part of these DJ DELF Dailies: the variety. Rather than doing the same, mundane classroom opener every single day, the Dailies have four completely different types of Bell Work challenges. Even if you do not teach French, I would recommend checking out the two week trial package. It includes ten Bell Work videos, all the activity recording tools, and the assessment and evaluation pieces. Scan the QR code to check them out.

Variety and consistency are the keys to effective Bell Work, and yes, you can have both. Here are a variety of Bell Work options that you can offer your students as a class-opening challenge:

- **Subject of the Day:** Provide students with a general or curriculum specific topic and have them write about it. Then, have students share and discuss.
- **Riddle of the Day:** Have students work individually or in small groups on a challenging riddle related to your subject.
- **Image of the Day:** Post an image. Have students analyse it, record, and then discuss their thoughts.
- **Song of the Day:** Choose a song tied to your current unit of study. Have the students analyse the music and lyrics.
- **Equation of the Day:** Let's get into some numeracy. Provide a math word problem related to your current course of study.

- **All Hands on Deck:** Using Legos or hands-on tools, have students work in groups to make creations or solve a problem.
- **Science Time:** Do an online search for some simple, creative science experiments students can do in pairs or small groups.
- **Read and Reason:** Choose a text for your students to read. Include questions that make them think deeper.
- **What's in the Box:** Place a hard-to-guess item in a box and play a game of 21 questions with your students.
- **Know the News:** Have students read or watch a video clip from a current news piece. Have them record their thoughts and then discuss as a class. Alternatively, find "ten years ago today" or "50 years ago today" news pieces or video clips.
- **Daily Diary:** Have students keep an active learning log.
- **Rockin' Review:** Display a question or problem that students have to solve that is directly related to yesterday's lesson.

Consistency is key in your delivery of Bell Work. Don't do Bell Work just some of the time, do it all of the time. Bell Work is the promissory note that more good learning is to come, because you've started the day ready to rock their learning. Bell Work announces to your students that you're organized and ready to go; a routine is already established.

To me, teaching without a prepared Bell Work activity is like pulling a truck out of the mud with a bungee cord: I guess it'll work eventually, but why work harder than you must?

Routines root teens. Routines also root pre-teens, adults, infants, and senior citizens. Routines can also route teens down the road to better learning habits. So, rock your routine from start to finish, my Teacher-Rockstar friends!

SET THE STAGE

ROCKIN' REASON

Role playing and simulating real-life situations related to your course curriculum will engage students and prepare them for when they leave the classroom and enter the real world.

ROCKIN' REQUIREMENTS

- ✓ Imagination
- ✓ Props
- ✓ Old, clean clothes
- ✓ Curriculum content

TEACHER TOOLS ARE LIKE MUSICAL EQUIPMENT

THE MORE TOOLS AVAILABLE, THE MORE YOUR LESSONS WILL BE FINE TUNED

Sometimes people ask me what it's like to perform live on stage, having thousands of people singing your songs or screaming your (stage) name. Bottomline: it's cool. It's a blessing, but it isn't real. I learned in university psychology class about the term "idealization." It's when we raise people high up on a pedestal, or when we view someone or something as perfect or as having exaggerated, positive qualities. Essentially, it means being starstruck. Fortunately, I understand how all that works. I know that as soon as maybe five minutes after the show, everyone moves on with their lives. A few songs may be stuck in people's heads, but they get back to checking their phones and resuming their normal lives. For those moments when I'm on stage: sure, it's fun. I play the role of the rockstar. The audience plays the role of the fans.

Role-playing for the sake of learning can be very effective. One time, at a concert in Burnaby, British Columbia, Canada, it backfired on me in front of two thousand fans. In the early 2000s, I wrote a song called "Le bleu de tes yeux" (translated: The Blue In Your Eyes). Boy bands were at the height of popularity, and I wanted to make my own sickly sweet love song. The plan was to add the song to my concert playlist as a nice, quiet break from all the loud, high-energy rock, rap, and electronic music normally experienced at an Étienne concert. To make it more fun, I decided that I would go into the audience and sing this French love song to French teachers. I asked the students to point out where their French teachers were seated, and I would my make way through the audience (even up into the second and third balconies) role-playing as a boy band member singing to their teachers. Without fail, students would rat out their teachers, vigorously pointing out exactly where they were hiding. I'd go up to a French teacher, sing a line or two, their students would go crazy, and then I would move onto the next teacher. This worked well. I executed this well-orchestrated plan without a hitch for years until things changed that fateful day in Burnaby.

I arrived at the foot of a French teacher that thought she would help me out by doing some role-playing of her own. She decided to play the role of a starstruck fan. Problem was I had no idea in advance. I went to one knee to begin singing the next line of the song, and the teacher jumped out of her chair onto my leg (picture Santa Claus at the mall) and began running her hands through my hair and hugging me. I was frozen. I kept singing, not daring to move. I could do nothing but wait until her role-playing segment was done. Funniest part: the press was in attendance at the show.

The next morning, in the only tabloid-esque article ever written about me, one newspaper printed an article highlighting the moment where a fan "decided that she was going to be the one making all the moves" and shared "a few seconds of awkward intimacy" with Étienne (Maple Ridge Times, April 6, 2005).

The only reason I knew that this article had appeared in the press was because, the next day, I performed a concert in Vancouver, British Columbia, and had people asking me all about it. As a result of this role playing incident gone awry, I didn't perform that song live in concert for another ten years. Now, when I role-play in concerts, I keep a safe distance from fans.

Fortunately, role-playing in the classroom is much safer. All your classroom is a stage and your students are merely players.

When I was a student, assessment and evaluation meant that you had a test at the end of a unit. That was it. I'm not saying that giving tests is a bad thing, but I am saying that today, we have many more ideas for summative evaluation at our fingertips. We can allow students at the end of a unit to show knowledge via the simulation of real-life experiences. Doesn't that just make sense?

I call them Big Ideas. These are projects or final tasks that students will have to complete, present, or perform at the end of a unit study. All these will set the stage for reachable success.

Let's look at some final projects that students can do individually:

- **Photo Fantastic:** If a picture tells a thousand words, surely your students can come up with twenty still photos with captions that capture the essence of all concepts learned during the unit study. Display final photos like an art gallery exposition and have students explain their work. Ex. Photos could lay out a process or steps of understanding of a math equation.
- **My Menu:** This delicious twist for an end project asks students to create and present unit concepts learned in the form of special dishes. Ex. Dish - Photosynthesis Soup. Description - Enjoy a little taste of sunlight energy. Key soup ingredients include glucose from carbon dioxide and water. Leaves just a hint of an oxygen aftertaste.
- **Diary of a Learner:** Students are required to write at least five journal entries during the course of the unit study. The last entry is designed to neatly tie things up. Having students re-explain what they've learned in their own words is powerful. For example, Diary of a Geographer: During the course of a unit on rocks, students would write five entries. The first entry would cover the unit introduction, the next three would each treat igneous, metamorphic, and sedimentary rocks, and the last entry would tie everything together. An alternative would be to have students convert journal entries into vlogs.
- **Monumental Moment:** Students create a monument or monuments that represent concepts learned in a unit of study. Each monument must have a prepared description. Students can film or present a mini-documentary on their monuments. For example, in history, monuments could be made out of clay or playdough to represent key historical figures.

Here are some final projects or big ideas for groups of two to five students:

- **Talk Show:** Students create a talk show where the host invites experts in the field of the current unit of study. For example, when studying Shakespeare's Hamlet in English class, the host can get the real side of the story from Hamlet, Claudia, Gertrude, Polonius, and a surprise guest appearance from the Ghost of Hamlet's Father. Through guest dialogue, students will be able to show knowledge of the play.
- **Movie Dub:** Students choose a two to five minute scene from a movie and hit the mute button. Each student plays the role of an actor from the film. The original lines from the film are replaced with a fact-filled conversation learned from the current course of study. This project can be presented live or can be filmed. Hint: animated movies are easier to work with in terms of dubbing voices over the muted original lines.
- **Amnesia:** Perfect for two students, or one — I forget. The first student is suffering from amnesia, while the other student is trying to fill the first in on what they've missed during the unit course of study. The student with amnesia asks a lot of questions and is shocked and in awe of all they missed. The second student is excited to share more. Hint: students can add props and costumes to make the skit look more authentic.
- **Great Debate:** Students prepare a script, film, or perform a live debate that covers the concepts learned in the current unit of study. Hint: divide students into four teams and host two mini-debates.
- **News Report:** Students can film or perform a live telecast of a complete news report centered around the concepts learned in units studied. Students can provide each concept as a headline, a weather report, a sports score, a political commentary, a movie review, a short interview, and more. Hint: students should create a real setting of a newsroom including props like tables, microphones, and video screens.

Of course, there's nothing stopping you from still having a traditional unit test after they're done their final Big Idea project. These skits or projects would only help reinforce concepts learned and help produce better results on those tests.

> They say that as teachers, we control the narrative.
> To right the script and to write the script, are imperative.

Set the stage for assessment and evaluation that will get your students writing scripts and role playing. By being in the act of acting, presenting, and role playing, students are getting to show their knowledge while practicing what are often authentic life situations. This tip may be outside of the traditional box, but it could unbox inspiration in a way you've never experienced before.

THAT'S A RAP

ROCKIN' REASON

Roses are red, violets are blue.
When you rhyme or rap a lesson,
Pedagogical dreams come true.

ROCKIN' REQUIREMENTS

- ✓ Internet
- ✓ Course content
- ✓ Pen
- ✓ Rhyming dictionary
- ✓ Paper
- ✓ Student beat-box rhythm section

GLOSSARY OF TEACHER-ROCKSTAR PARALLELS

PLANNING IS LIKE SONGWRITING

It takes time to make a classic, but done properly, students will forever be singing the chorus.

"Can you freestyle rap?" That's a question I've heard many times from my students and from fans. Fortunately, I do have a few go-to "freestyle" rhymes that I can bust out when needed. One of them became the basis to my song "Pourquoi Take French?". Freestyle rappers spend a lot of time practicing 4 to 16 line raps that they can incorporate into any impromptu rap battle. Rap is popular because it usually incorporates rhyme. Rhyme tickles the ear and causes the listener to pay attention. This is why I've been putting lessons to rhyme since my days in teachers college.

The very first educational song that I wrote was a rap. I was in teachers college and the night before class, I remembered that we had a lesson plan due the next morning. Stuck for a better idea, I wrote a rap about farm animals and the noises they make. I presented it live to the instructor and to my classmates, and they loved it. Some even began to immediately rap along to the chorus. I got an A+ on that assignment and, more importantly, I learned that I had a forever, go-to lesson plan: simply rap about what you want your students to learn.

Putting together a curriculum rap is not as hard as it may seem. All you need to do is take a look at the keywords of a unit study and see what kind of sweet rhymes and fantastic flows you can assemble. The great thing about rap is that you can actually make a story or even a conversation out of it.

If the only rapping you do involves gift wrap around the holidays, have your students make the raps for you. Give them upcoming keywords to your unit and have them look up the meaning while trying to make up a poem or rap. Again, rap is simply poetry put to a beat. If you feel that your students may not know what poetry really is, share this rap that I made about poetry. This is a perfect example of this chapter's tip. It teaches everything students are supposed to learn about poetry in elementary school:

All About Poetry

Whether you think it's for the better or for the worse
A poem doesn't have to rhyme; free verse
These words, you'll know them, they help make a poem
Put words together for your friends and show them
Poems come in many forms for many pallets;
Like haiku, sonnet, free verse and ballads
The rhythm or metre is the beat of the lines
The predictable rhythm that the poem defines
Rhyming patterns vary: AB, CB, AA, BB / There are plenty
Shakespeare wrote fourteen-line poems called sonnets
With paper he put set rhyme schemes on it
A ballad is a poem in songlike form
Found short and narrative is quite the norm
Free verse is a common form of poetry
It may or may not rhyme it's a modern style, you see
Haiku; seventeen syllables, in a three-line form
To a five-seven -five pattern it must conform
Poetry doesn't have many rules
But, here is a list of some useful tools
Alliteration, metaphor, repetition,
Onomatopoeia, simile, personification
Alliteration, like rhyme, is a repetition of sound
The first letters of words are where it's often found
Repetition is used to make its point (repeat 2x)
Onomatopoeia uses words to imitate
Like bang or plop its imagery relates
Personification gives human qualities
To an animal, object or conceptualities
Similes make comparisons in poems using as or like
Metaphors compare without these words
(Example) "I'm the biker and the bike."

Scan the QR code to access the music video to this song.

Are you feeling like the rap should come from you, the teacher, but you're nervous about rapping in person? No problem. Create a rap and record it, even if it's just on audio. If you're ready, willing, and able, shoot your own mini music video performing your rap creation. You'll have a teaching tool that you can use for the rest of your career. Put that video up on any social media platform and watch it go viral. Who knows? We may be touring together in the near future!

Hand out the words to your rap and have students listen to your audio while reading along. Perform your rap live while select students lay down the rhythm via some sweet beatboxing. You can also find some good beats by searching "instrumental beats" on any online video platform. Encourage the entire class to rap along. Film a music video together as a class.

Take this rap, for example. I put it together to start a unit on the periodic table. It's about an angry pirate confronting a potential thief. The weirder the better, my fellow Teacher-Rockstars! It recites very much like a cheerleader cheer.

> A-R, A-R. Pirate says, "Something's wrong!"
> A-R, A-R "My treasures all argon"
> A-U. Hey you! Is that my necklace made of gold?
> A-G, Hey Gee! "No, this one's sliver. It's just old."

Don't feel like you have the rhythm to do this freestyle? Borrow some melodies that your students are familiar with and syllabically replace the original words with keywords and definitions from your unit study. Here are four ways that you can do that:

- Syllabically cover the chorus of a current, popular song like I did in the chapter tip for "Keep Up." Try to choose a song that most or all of your students will recognize. That connection will make your creation more effective.

- Syllabically cover the chorus to a classic song. Take the verse and chorus of "We Will Rock You" by Queen and teach regular -ER verbs in French:

  Pour JE tu mets un E, et TU E-S, et E pour IL et ELLE aussi
  (Buddy, you're a boy, make a big noise. Playing in the street, gonna be a big man someday)
  NOUS O-N-S, VOUS E-Z, ILS et ELLES sont E-N-T
  (You got mud on your face, you big disgrace. Kicking your can all over the place)
  Mots d'action en E-R. Hey! E-R. Hey! Mots d'action en E-R.
  (We will, we will rock you. Hey! Rock you,   Hey! We will, we will, rock you!)

- Syllabically cover the melody to a popular commercial jingle. Math teachers might appreciate this little tune. Use the Kit Kat® chocolate bar commercial jingle to teach BEDMAS:

  Brackets go first, exponents go next,
  (Give me a break.   Give me a break.)
  Division, multiplication, we're not done yet.
  (Break me off a piece of the KitKat® bar)
  Addition adds up, subtraction is last.
  (Give me a break.   Give me a break.)
  Now you know the order of BEDMAS.
  (Break me off a piece of the KitKat® bar)

- Syllabically cover the chorus to a nursery rhyme. Take the nursery rhyme for "Mary Had A Little Lamb" and use it to teach the parts of a microscope. Students sing, touching each part:

  Focus, arm and eyepiece lens, the stage clips, objective lens,
  (Mary had a little lamb, little lamb, little lamb)
  Nose piece, light source, head and stage, illuminator, base.
  (Mary had a little lamb, her fleece was white as snow)

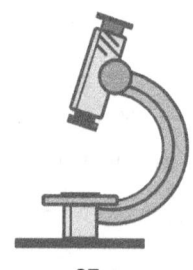

UNDERCOVER AGENT

ROCKIN' REASON

Today, you're not just a teacher. You're an undercover agent. Get in character to make learning more real for your students.

ROCKIN' REQUIREMENTS

- ✓ Costumes
- ✓ Props
- ✓ Masks
- ✓ Makeup
- ✓ Course content

When people ask me about my most significant memories from my years of touring, I often think about one particular concert: between the first and second songs, students in the first two rows to my right started screaming "Étienne" super loudly to catch my attention. I looked over and one of the students yelled, "Now!" Simultaneously, they all shut their eyes. They had all put Étienne temporary tattoos on their eyelids. I was staring at about 20 faces with 40 Étienne tattoos instead of eyeballs. It was partly spooky but mostly flattering. After the show, I made it a point to head down over to where they were seated, sign some autographs, and take a photo with these creative people.

Earlier on in my music career, the press labeled me as the "Eminem of educational music." The media cited the parallels of catchy refrains and loud concert experiences. Oddly enough, we are roughly the same age and did grow up 8 miles from each other, but I'm not sure if there's much more there than that. However, I do think the press exposed an important fact: when I'm onstage, it's like I'm another person. It's like I'm playing a character. I've often credited my younger years of watching pro wrestling for much of my persona and stage presence. "Étienne" is a larger-than-life character onstage. He connects with and edutains (educationally entertains) the crowd.

Some things work better when undercover. When I'm onstage, I'm an undercover teacher: a teacher disguised as a rockstar. Think of all the superheroes that work undercover (Superman/Clark Kent, Batman/Bruce Wayne). In the classroom, we can do the same. We can essentially be anything we want to be. Dress up in costume as something related to your unit of study. Studying animals? Dress up like an animal. Studying elements of the periodic table? Dress up as an elemental superhero displaying the power of that element. Reading a novel? Dress up as one of the main characters. Teaching Math? Dress up like a calculator. Sharing a song? Throw on some shades, grab a pen for a microphone, and lip-sync your heart out.

My students tend to learn best from characters. They're influenced by social media celebrities, musicians, actors, and the like. It stands to reason that they can also be influenced by characters in the classroom. Unlike other tips in this book that encourage students to step into the spotlight, this tip highlights you. This is your chance to catch their attention with attire.

I came up with the idea of playing a character when I found myself forced to teach grade 10 history to French Immersion students. How was I going to fill in for the real history teacher? Their history teacher was on maternity leave, and I thought it would be rude to ask her to come back and help me. Unlike other subject areas where I could bring in living experts, all the key players in history are, well, dead. What was I to do? Gather the children for a séance to invoke spiritual sessions with the history makers of the past?

We started by learning the who in this huge history text before learning the when, what, why, or how. Many subject areas have whos. Science has scientists. Math has mathematicians. Language has authors and poets. Music has composers and songwriters. Allow your students to discover these colorful characters before learning of their accomplishments and impact. By allowing students to learn what they did to make this world a brighter place, you make their minds a brighter place. Allow students to meet the icons of your subject area. By knowing the key figures responsible for what we know about a specific subject area, students can begin to better understand from where the ideas, facts, and teachings come.

Never dressing up to help your students learn is like wearing white during a snowstorm (Figure 1): it means you'll never stand out. To use a musical comparison, never taking a chance to try this tip is like being a guitar without strings: sure, it's still a guitar, but dressing it up with some strings is how you can really make some music. So, go to that closet of yours, your friend's closet, or make a run to the local thrift store and show your students that you're 100% invested in their learning by rocking some curriculum-related attire! After all, we have the freedom of wearing whatever clothes, outfits or costumes we desire.

Figure 1 - Teacher wearing all white in a snowstorm

VOILINS IN THE CLASS

ROCKIN' REASON

We need more violins in the classroom. Music soothes the soul. Music can grab students by their hearts and create a perfect learning environment.

ROCKIN' REQUIREMENTS

- ✓ Computers
- ✓ Internet access
- ✓ Electronic devices
- ✓ An ear for what soothes
- ✓ Speakers
- ✓ Music selection

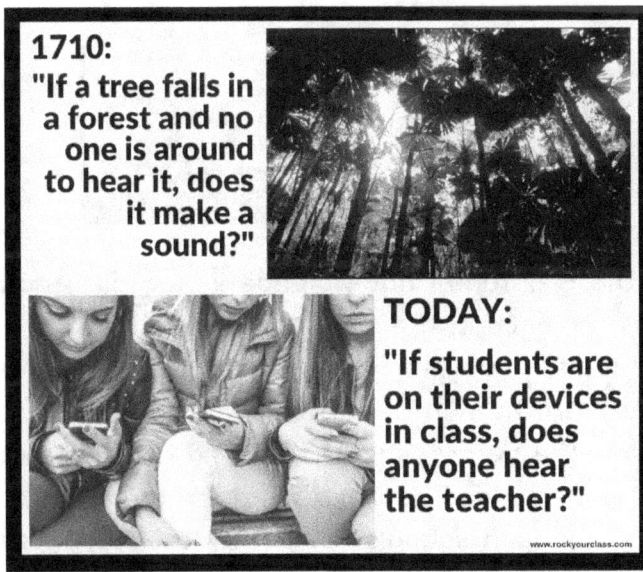

1710: "If a tree falls in a forest and no one is around to hear it, does it make a sound?"

TODAY: "If students are on their devices in class, does anyone hear the teacher?"

www.rockyourclass.com

One thing that I've learned over the years is that music is incredibly powerful. It's the background of our lives, the voice of celebration, and it can take you to places you've never imagined. In 2007, while touring in Australia, I was asked to add one more show to the tour. I was asked if I could squeeze in a show for students in the northwestern town of Quairading. What I didn't know was that the show would turn out to be anything but typical. When I arrived, I found out that I would be performing at the town hall. After the concert, I learned that Quairading was celebrating its 100th anniversary. They took me and my family out for a meal where I learned that I'd been asked to perform there as a part of the town's 100th year celebration event. They said that they wanted music to be a part of their celebration, and I had the honor of bringing that music.

Violins in the classroom, not violence in the classroom. If you want to talk violence in the classroom I can share some stories: I've taught at a school where the number of suspensions per year was greater than the number of students. I've taught at schools where I knew the parole officers by name because students on my sports teams had to check in with them before practices and games. I've taught in schools where we lost students to drugs and alcohol, schools where students would get arrested for crimes like swarming and grand theft auto, and those were just the elementary schools. Don't even get me started on the high schools. You can say that I've earned some "classroom cred" having to teach at some challenging schools, but I wouldn't change any of my school placements. I've always cared about the students no matter where I was teaching.

I believe that there's an argument that more violins could help curb tendencies for violence in the classroom. I've seen the power of music, not just from the stage. It's awe-inspiring how music can take the audience from one emotion to another. More effectively, I've seen the same awe-inspiring results in the school and classroom. Two things that I've noticed over my career when it comes to students and music:

1. Music affects mood.
2. It's undeniable that the better a student's mood is before class begins, the better the chance they'll succeed during class.

Beat them to the punch. Strike at the heart of your students as soon as class time begins. If my students are engaged in Bell Work or working quietly at their desks, I'll often play music. This is one of my favorite instrumental albums to play. The album "Valor" from Ichos Music is perfect because it lasts 38 minutes long and takes you on a musical journey. Scan the QR code to access the YouTube link:

My students say they feel like they're in a video game when I play it. The music is soothing and triumphant. Perfect for when students need to concentrate on work. The music stops students from talking to each other and seems to snap them right into work mode. What's great about using instrumental music like this is that I don't have to worry about proofreading lyrics.

If you think it works great in the classroom, you should see the effect music has in the hallways. If your school is having issues with attendance, loitering, or poor student conduct in the hallways, ask your administration to play soothing, classical music before and after classes. You'll never see students move so fast to get to their classes.

Once students arrive in the classroom, set the music mood. Does it always have to be soothing classical or epic instrumental music? Surely not. Mix up styles of music you play while students work on tasks. Type these keywords into any online music or video platform and choose your tunes:

- Classical music
- Orchestral dubstep instrumental
- Gregorian chant dubstep instrumental
- Jazz instrumental
- Piano instrumental
- Electronica instrumental
- Celtic instrumental music
- Quiet night sounds
- Babbling brook sounds

Yes, the last two may not be music, but they represent another avenue of positive, mood-changing sounds that can turn your classroom into a symphony of satisfied learners.

WHY OH WHY ?

ROCKIN' REASON

Knowing is half the battle. If students know why they're in your classroom to learn, you've already bridged a huge gap towards understanding.

ROCKIN' REQUIREMENTS

- ✓ Computers
- ✓ Internet access
- ✓ Pen
- ✓ Course content
- ✓ Paper
- ✓ Electronic devices

Student voices are like microphones

Let them take a stand and be heard.

You have no idea how many people have asked me the question, "Why?" Why did you choose to become a teacher and a musician? Why be a Teacher-Rockstar? Why not be one or the other? Why did you become Étienne?

Becoming Étienne really wasn't by choice. What I didn't explain in the introduction of this book is how I ended up at that fateful French teacher meeting where I was labelled with the stage-name "Étienne." Let me explain why I was there.

It was my first year out of Teachers College, and I was covering a maternity leave for a French teacher from September 1st to the end of February. It was already February, and I had to start thinking ahead: I needed another job. After all, I had become accustomed to paying bills and eating food, and I wanted to continue that trend. Knowing that there were no other long-term positions available for the rest of the year, I'd be relegated to the day-to-day supply teacher list.

I don't know how it works in your school district, but at this particular district — it was the teachers' responsibility to find a substitute teacher if they were going to be ill or needed a day off for an appointment. There were no automated phone or online systems. It was not the responsibility of the school district. It was your responsibility to find a qualified teacher to replace you for the day.

Soon out of a job, it was important that I let the French teachers of our district know that I could be a capable substitute should they need me for a day. I asked the French Consultant, Elaine Marentette, if I could have five minutes during the meeting to address the teachers and convince them that their students would be in capable hands. I wanted to show them that I was fun and flexible. I decided that the best way for them to remember me was to play for them two French songs that I had composed for my students over the past few months while I was covering the maternity leave. I played the first song, the teachers sang along, and things were looking up. I played the second song and the French teachers were all smiles. I proceeded to pass along my name and contact information to all the teachers in attendance. No one was interested. All they wanted to know was if they could get a copy of those two songs, and if I had any more. It was at that time that the French Consultant translated my given name of Steven, exclaiming, "We have our own rockstar right here. It's Étienne!"

Fun fact: I didn't get a single phone call as a supply teacher. Not one. One month after that meeting, I moved school districts and took a job to cover another maternity leave for the rest of that school year, but I did oblige those wonderful teachers. I promptly went to work putting the only five songs that I had onto a cassette tape. I made multiple copies and distributed them to those teachers. Within weeks, I began receiving phone calls from school districts all over Ontario asking for copies of my album. Album? What album? Word of mouth had spread to the point that people actually thought I was a rockstar or something. That summer, I had to make a decision: either go ahead and make a real album or start kindly telling people, "Umm, no. I'm a teacher, not a rockstar, but thanks anyway."

That summer, after a lot of thought and prayer, I took all the money I had to my name ($500), and found a recording studio that would help me make my first album. That was how it started, and now you know the "why."

"Why?" is the most common question that teachers hear in the classroom. Our students always want to know why. Why do we have to do this? Why are we doing this? Why are we here? Do these questions sound familiar? They may sound like questions purposely posed by students to derail a lesson plan, but they're not. These are important questions. Students simply want to know what connection your planned lesson will have with who they are and what they will become. They're truly asking why.

My favorite teachers were the ones that left no questions as to why we were learning a lesson. My physics teacher, Mr. Fay, was always adept at this. I remember when he was teaching us the principle of inertia, he looked at me from across the room and saw that I was not understanding the lesson. He said, "Steve, you know why you need to learn the principle of inertia? When you're going on a date, should you arrive at the destination turning left or right? Think about it. You're in the driver seat and she's beside you. If you're heading straight and you make a left turn, where does she go? What happens if you make a right turn? Exactly!" How cool was he? He knew that I wasn't interested in physics, but it was no secret I liked girls. He hit me where I was at. He gave me a reason to learn inertia (the "why").

Inspired by Mr. Fay, I make sure to always let me students know why we're learning what we're learning. I even wrote a song for my French students to lay out exactly why they should be learning French in my classroom and how it will benefit them in more ways than they could possibly imagine. This song went viral. Why? Because, it simply tells it like it is. The best response to the question "why" is the plain and simple truth. Check out this song. I encourage you to write a rap for your students about your subject area, or better yet, have them write the rap themselves. Record their version and play it for other classes for years to come.

Pourquoi Take French?

Pourquoi take French? I heard you ask. Well sit back and relate as I kick your aspirations into gear. You got nothing to fear. When you learn a second language, opportunities appear. I know many languages, I'm having fun. A lot more than I would be, if I stuck with one. Yeah, I learned French in school, not in my home. Mais je parle français wherever I may roam. Yeah, I've been to Rome, Barcelona and France. Rocked the masses down under, watched them bounce and dance. But, enough about me, let me talk about you. You gotta a choice, it's your voice. Watcha gonna do? You can open cash doors, your value soars. When you learn a second language, man, the world is yours. Let me tell ya little story I think you might like. It's about my High School friend whose name is Mike. He said "Pourquoi take French? I don't live in France!" So, he didn't take French, although he had the chance. So, check it, then one day he meets up with the girl of his dreams, a rare beauty like the ones up on the movie screens. He walks up to her and says "Shawty, how do you do?" She says, "Je parle français. Parlez-vous?" He went from geekin' to freakin, he couldn't be speakin' the French that would win him the girl he was meetin'. So, he turned to me, for French help he was seeking. He nearly flipped his lid. I'll tell you what I did. I walked up to her and said "Bonjour" and now we got three kids. Over 200 million people speak French in this world. In more than 50 different countries, that's lotsa boys and girls. French is the official language of UN and NATO, the Red Cross, the Olympics, and UNESCO. So, the moral of the story, is just this: it's not about the money-making or taking all them trips. But ya say, I'm gonna be a doctor, lawyer, engineer. Well, those cats make more money when they speak French my dear. 'Cause the world is multilingual, it's real not virtual. And you'll be jammin' to these words I flow. Just stick to what you know fo' sho'. Whether for business or for pleasure, learning French unlocks a treasure. With no value you can measure, you'll be rich man. Yeah, forever.

Scan the QR code below to watch the official music lyric video for this song for some more inspiration when you try your own.

It's a lot easier than you think. Simply take your curriculum content and make a rap about it. Here are a couple of pre-made raps I made for math, science, and geography from the top of my head. I made these in just a few minutes. You can probably do much better with a bit of time and effort.

MATH
Yo it's me (Enter your teacher name here), I'm on a mission
To teach you more than multiplication and division.
Math is found in everything you do;
Subtract your doubts, I'll add it up for you.
Math is found in simple things, every day,
Every time you count, measure or weigh.
Math rules the world, it ain't even funny,
You can bank on the fact, you even use it with money.
So pay attention in class, as we calculate;
Math is what makes this world so great.

SCIENCE (Elements of the Periodic Table)
Hey you! Au! That necklace is Gold
Not Silver, you see, that would be Ag
Which, of course, is better than Carbon, C,
If made of Copper, I'd say Cu later my friend
And disappear. O? Like Oxygen.
Are you? Ru? Ruth Enium?
Who travelled far from Fr, Francium?
I heard Lithium is sick. Is that Li?
If so I have some sage advice:
If He is sick, Helium. If he B dead, Barium
Or know some doctors? Cm. Maybe they'll Curium.

GEOGRAPHY
Hungary, I was Russian to Finnish
A well-prepared Turkey dish.
Then all of a Sudan Iran in my socks
Until I tripped and fell over Iraq.
It hurt so bad, I thought I was a Ghana,
So I visited a doctor in Tijuana.

I actually got carried away with the Geography one. Here are some lines that were just too corny to include in my Geography rap. When working with students, can teachers really be too corny?

GEOGRAPHY (the rejected lines)
Taiwan to Spain the rest of my life with you!
You Malta my heart! York make everything New.
My love for you Israel! My heart is now carried.
Jamaica me happy. Guyana get married?
Norway I can live without you. Syria-ously!

This tip should not be restricted to the "why" of your overall subject area. Students will always benefit if they know why they're learning a particular lesson or unit, as well. Never keep the "why" a mystery. To ensure that my students know why, I always begin units of study by having them choose the project or Big Idea of the unit before we even begin. When students know the final project before we even start, there's never any reason to ask why we are doing any of the scaffolded steps or stages that lead to the end of the unit. They should be able to see, or at least trust, that it all fits in together.

If a journey of a thousand miles begins with a single step, then a journey of understanding begins with a single question: why?

XPERT HELP IS HERE

ROCKIN' REASON

You can't know everything. Let others share their expertise with you and your students.

ROCKIN' REQUIREMENTS

✓ Guest speakers   ✓ Internet access

✓ Willingness to share classroom time

Connecting with the audience is a powerful experience, but one of the coolest experiences that I've had in my years of touring came offstage. My family and I had arrived in Nelson, New Zealand to start a nationwide tour, but we didn't know anything about their beautiful country. We were tourists, outsiders, and unaware of the country's heritage, culture, and customs. We had yet to make a connection, but it wouldn't be long.

Our first day in Nelson, my family and I were honored to be greeted with our own Māori welcoming ceremony courtesy of our New Zealand hosts. Part of that ceremony involved the hongi, a traditional Māori greeting whereby each of Māori men, faces ornate in the coolest tattoos I'd ever seen, came one by one standing forehead to forehead, nose to nose, and breath to breath with me as they recited their welcoming words. This type of ceremony is often reserved for visiting royalty or dignitaries. It was quite the honor that I'll never forget. It was later explained to me that in the hongi, the ha (meaning: breath of life) is exchanged as a symbolic show of unity and connection.

We learn from experiences and we can learn from others who have stories to tell of their own experiences. The more voices that you can add to your students' learning experience, the better. Same goes for onstage. We ran a touring festival called Frenchstock for a few years and travelled all over Canada and the United States. We had many musicians and even a magician on the tour. We were performers with different voices, but we shared the same message.

From left to right: Marc Tardif, Michelle White, Christine Atallah, Étienne

Whether in person or online, guest speakers can make a huge impression. In the late 2010s, I used to frequent an online platform for teachers called the French Playground. There, my students were involved in online meetings and interviews with French authors, actors, athletes, historians, and musicians. The bonus of connecting with these guests was that my students benefited from interacting with native French speakers, all of whom spoke with a slightly different French accent.

Today, we don't need ready-made, online platforms like these. Guest speakers are easy to find. They can even be a colleague that is on a prep period. If they have no experience in your subject area, no problem. They can play the role of a character from a novel or historical figure. Just provide them with a script to follow.

A word of advice though: you wouldn't hire someone claiming to be a musician because they told you they could play the radio, would you? Find real experts. Students can spot a phony. These experts are representing you, your lesson, and your subject area.

Guest speakers that can be great for your students:

- Politicians for social studies class
- Accountants for math class
- Athletes for physical education class
- Actors for drama class
- Authors for English and other classes
- Lab technician for science class
- Travel agent for geography class
- Museum curator for history class
- Doctor or nurse for health class
- Local artist for visual arts class
- Local musician for music class
- Local cook or nutritionist for foods class
- Seamstress for fashion class
- College or university professors for any subject area

There is another side to this "xpert" thing: allowing yourself to learn from experts in order to return to the classroom with their expertise. Expert help is meant for you, as well. Professional support means you never have to feel like you're an island unto yourself. You can find support from:

- Your curriculum
- Your school board consultant for your teachable area
- School administration
- Department chair
- Your union
- Colleagues
- Friends from teachers college
- Blogs
- Vlogs
- Podcasts
- Books
- Conferences
- Social media (follow popular teachers or join teacher groups)

A common thread with all the tips in this book is the idea of making connections. No matter the teaching or learning strategy, the underlying focus is to engage students more in their learning and to strengthen the sense of trust and team between you and your students.

YUCK! MARKING!

ROCKIN' REASON

Understanding how to evaluate and how to manage marking are keys to a successful teaching career.

ROCKIN' REQUIREMENTS

✓ Food

✓ A good book

✓ Free time

✓ A plan

✓ Understanding of the assignments-marked to rewards ratio

Rockstars get evaluated by the press and by the general public. One of the places rockstars are evaluated is at award shows. Award shows are kind of like the yearly graduation ceremony for all artists that have produced work that given year. Award shows can be exciting and nerve-racking. I think the coolest thing about them is getting to meet other artists backstage. Students and fans alike ask me, "Have you ever met anyone really famous? Like real musicians?" Great question! I have.

I've had the privilege of rubbing shoulders with some great Canadian artists over the years. Actually, I've met just as many in airports due to frequent touring. Secret: if you keep your eyes open the next time you're at an airport, look at the waiting areas of destinations to large, popular cities. You may be surprised who you find there. I have met and spoken with actors, rockstars, and even Yo-Yo Ma. No, not the famous rapper. That's Yo-Yo Momma. I mean the famous cellist. I actually sat with him on my way to a concert in Wisconsin, USA. Great guy. So, keep your eyes open when travelling. You never know who might be in the seat next to you.

Let's get back to being evaluated at awards shows. How do rockstars get evaluated? That depends on the award show. Musicians have to enter their work in order to be considered. Some awards are determined behind-the-scenes, and the politics would make your head spin. My publicist always submitted my work to awards shows that were transparent. For example, the one award show, where I twice won "Canada's Artist of the Year" in the Children's Music category, relies on national voting. As teachers, we should be open and transparent in how we evaluate. Students should know exactly what we're looking for and how to meet curriculum expectations.

Teacher-Rockstar tips don't have to be exclusive to just teaching and learning strategies. Planning out how we evaluate is just as important as planning out a rockin' lesson plan. I've learned that I can be just as creative with my evaluation and with the way I mark assignments.

Marking? Yuck! What is your aim when it comes time to mark? I have some ideas about assessment that I'm confident will leave a mark. Mark my words. I know that assessment and evaluation is important, but it can be tedious and extremely time-consuming. Let's examine three different ways to shake up the way you spend your time marking tests and assignments:

- **Vary your forms of assessment and evaluation.** Before you get to your marking, consider if you'll be marking for summative, formative, diagnostic, norm-referenced, criterion-referenced, or some other form of evaluation. Decide if you're going to evaluate through written, oral, or task-based methods. If all you give are tests and quizzes in the same way, chances are you may get very tired of marking them. If you're choosing to provide a written form of assessment, decide what that will look like: multiple choice, true or false, short answer, essays, matching, charts, long answer, equations, fill-in-the-blank, definitions, replace words, organize terms, categorize, explain, and give opinions are just some possibilities.

- **Vary your marking routine.** What is your tests-marked to rewards-eaten ratio? If you're a Teacher-Rockstar, you know exactly what I'm talking about! Is it one scoop of ice cream for every ten tests marked? One chip for every test marked? One licorice stick for every complete section of tests marked? Food incentives are no stranger to the world of grading papers.

The most sane way I find to grade papers or tests is by chunking. Chunking with a chunk of chocolate in between each chunk is a gastronomically tasty idea. Marking all page ones first, then page twos, then page threes allows our brains to acclimatize to the whole process. When chunking, I find that sometimes it's best to mark the more tedious sections first and get them out of the way. "To-Do pile/Done pile" is another method. Teachers can get a sly satisfaction watching the To-Do pile shrink and the Done pile grow. Some of my colleagues call this method "Dung-pile/Done pile." Because, when they look at the former, they see a crap-ton of marking to do! My more politically correct colleagues call their piles the "To-Do/Ta-Da" piles. Once off the "To-Do" pile... Ta-Da! The marking disappears.

- **Don't peek. Let your students surprise you.** This technique is especially effective before that point in time where you start to recognize students by their handwriting. Try marking assignments and tests without knowing whose papers you're grading. When I was a student, I sometimes wondered if my teachers just looked at the name on the paper and gave a grade without even reading a word. You? One way of assuring your students that you don't do this is by using sticky notes. Before marking, grab a handy pack of sticky notes and cover students' names with these reusable wonders. After you're done all of your marking, remove and replace the sticky notes (who doesn't like recycling?) and note any surprises you see in the test results of some of your students. Make a mental note to offer them a word of praise or encouragement the next day. With this method, no one can ever question your fairness in evaluation.

ZEST TO COMPETE

ROCKIN' REASON

Teach to the competitive nature that lies strongly within a great majority of your students. Compete, compete, repeat.

ROCKIN' REQUIREMENTS

✓ Computers ✓ Course content

✓ Internet access ✓ Paper

✓ Electronic devices ✓ Willingness to organize

Face your failures.

THEN TURN YOUR BACK ON THEM AND MOVE FORWARD.

Sometimes, I feel like my students all come from the same nation: the nation of Procrasta. They hand in assignments late, and at times, they're very hard to motivate; however, I find that when I add a bit of competitive fun into the mix of my teaching, students become much more engaged in their learning.

We would have competitions to see how fast and how well we could sing French songs. Do you remember the song "Mots d'action en ER" (translation: Action Words With -ER Endings) that I talked about in the chapter, "That's A Rap"? I remember one time, I had a competition between all my grade 7 classes to see who could sing it the fastest. At the end of the song, I purposely omitted the last "Hey!" that students would normally shout out. This was designed so that the song would not end on a big chant of "Hey!" but instead a wall of silence. When getting caught up in the singing of the song, it's hard not to add an extra "Hey" even though it's not there.

Knowing that it was hard not to add that extra word, I decided to spice things up. I told each class that if they added the "Hey" at the end, their attempt at the school record would not count, even if they had broken it. Any extra "Hey" would negate the attempt. One instance, during the competition, an over-exuberant student in my period 3 class yelled out "Hey!" at the end of the song right as the class was on a record-crushing speedrun. One particularly competitive and larger boy in the class got angry with the loss of the record and yelled out, "Oh, Jason. Nice going! You're dead after school, man!" As a teacher, you could imagine how I felt. This warmed my heart! Imagine: my students were going to get together after school to discuss what we had done in French class that day. Success!

In the mid-1990s, I taught at a very sports-centric middle school. I tapped into my students' sense of competition at all times. We kept points, scores, and rankings for all sorts of games, contests, and daily activities. We even kept record of the class that handed out paper the fastest.

My most popular competition was Verbal Olympix. Verbal Olympix consisted of one-on-one competitions of French verb conjugation. Do you remember those projector wheels that I mentioned in the "Inspector Gadget" chapter? I took two of those wheels and attached them to a 2x4 plank of wood. The top wheel featured all kinds of subjects and pronouns. The bottom wheel showcased a wide variety of verbs. I leaned the contraption against the chalkboard and had one student stand on each side of the spinning device with chalk in hand. When both spinning wheels came to rest, the arrows indicated a subject and a verb. The first student to write the proper conjugation in a full sentence won the challenge. We would run bracketed competitions until we determined who were the four best students in each class.

Then, we would play "home" and "away" games for about a week. For the beginning first two minutes of class, four "away" students from a different period (ex. period 3) would come visit a "home" class of another period (ex. period 4). Those four students would play quick rounds of Verbal Olympix. I tracked the wins and losses. The "away" students loved that they were missing the first few minutes of their other periods in order to play these games. I was fortunate enough to have colleagues that permitted them the time to do so. At the end of the week, a winning class was announced. Then, the top students from each of my five classes were invited during lunch hour for the championship round on the last day of that week. My classroom was packed as the championship student was determined. At the end of every year, the Verbal Olympix winners (the reps from each class and the eventual student winner) would end up in the yearbook in the sports section between soccer and basketball. Yes, this yearly competition was heralded as equals to our two biggest sports.

There are many alternatives for this wheel-spinning game. Math teachers could have numbers on each wheel and alter the challenge and students could be asked to multiply, divide, add, or subtract the two numbers. Teachers from all subject areas can use one wheel and have key terms from a unit study printed on it. Spin the wheel and the first student to write the definition on the board wins.

You may be a bit surprised to learn that whenever I've had competitions in class, it's rarely been student vs. student. I prefer my whole class working together for a high score or record. I like having them competing against other classes for bragging rights, even against my classes from the past. That's right: my students strive to be the best ever, even against phantom classes. This creates a special level of positive competition, because the opponent isn't even real. By doing this, I'm avoiding any overzealous, competitive sentiment that might arise from class vs. class competition between classes of the same year.

Speaking of competition, if you ever feel, as a teacher, that you're competing against your students, pull a judo move. It's a classic case of, "If you can't beat 'em, join 'em." In judo, you use holds and leverage to unbalance the opponent. In this case, if you feel that your students are competing against the flow of your teaching strategies, use their flow to re-leverage their energy (even negative energy) with a spark of competition. Turn the tables to get the energy (now positive) flowing the way you want.

My students have so much fun in my classroom that they have no idea how much they're learning. Sometimes, I suspect that they believe that I'm "on their side," because they feel like we're avoiding the curriculum. By engaging in so many fun, hands-on, sometimes competitive activities, they think that I'm a liberator, a rebel, and a trailblazer.

One of the best ways to harness the energy of a hard-to-motivate class is via competition. Turn things up a notch. Take old trophies and convert them to championship trophies. Make a world heavyweight championship belt (like in pro wrestling) that only the student with the best record is allowed hold.

In terms of the best learning strategies: those that compete blow the competition away!

OUTRO

SHAKE UP LEARNING.
AMPLIFY ENGAGEMENT.
ROCK ENROLMENT.

Toronto, Ontario, Canada

Not too tipsy from all those tips yet? Get ready for a few more. Here are some last minute pieces of advice for teachers to live by:

- Sometimes teaching can be like drinking grape juice and expecting it to taste like fine wine. Good things take time. Take your time to get good. Be patient when trying out these A-Z tips and others that you discover along your pedagogical journey.
- Be patient with yourself and be reasonable with your expectations; both those of your students and those that you put on yourself.
- Winging it through your career does not a good teacher make. Winging it is a bull in the china shop approach. When teachers are careless, it can look like they care less.

My editors and proofreaders said to tone it down with all the corny puns in my book. The outro isn't really part of the book, right? Exactly! Here's everything that they said "no" to:

- When in Rome, do as the Romans, but when in the classroom, no one wants their students to be roamin'. So, keep them engaged using the tips found in this book and your students will be like paper, pen, and gift cards: stationary!
- Some pedagogical ideas are like gray hairs: they're meant to dye. Good teaching strategies aren't like queens and kings; they don't just come from out of the air, but they're developed from a complete realm of understanding your subjects.
- Open up your students' eyes to new ways of learning. Speaking of eyes, remember to always keep your students in eyesight. After all, they're your pupils, and without pupils, your eyes can't see what's really going on in the classroom. When it comes to student learning, remember this: if it ain't broke, don't fix it, but if they ain't woke, then fix it. Keep their learning eyes open.
- Teaching strategies are like darts: they may all have a point, but they need to be on target to really count. They're better when they hit the mark of matching curriculum needs with student interest.

The truest strategy that ties all these tips together is connection. Making connections is the key. Don't be an island unto yourself. Connect! If you've exhausted all options with colleagues in your area, please connect with me via the website named after this book: www.rockyourclass.com. You can keep up with my crazy blog, videos, and even hit me up for some Teacher-Rockstar curriculum shop talk.

Don't stop learning, learn to never stop, and most importantly: keep doing what you do to rock your class!

Yours in education,

About Étienne

Steven Langlois has spent the better part of three decades teaching K-12 in many subject areas while taking on various leadership roles as Department Head, Instructional Coach, Mentor and District Program Coordinator.

He has presented keynote addresses and workshop sessions at teacher conferences worldwide. As Étienne, he has performed sold-out French and Spanish educational shows in theatres and arenas across the globe, which has taught him exactly what it takes to motivate students of all ages.

He has worked as an author and consultant for leading educational publishing companies, learning the best practices of effective content creation.

Book ÉTIENNE for your school, district, faculty of education, or teacher conference

Étienne is a high-energy keynote and session speaker that empowers new educators and inspires even the weariest of veteran teachers.

Étienne brings his "A" game to every "STEAM" conference sharing authentic strategies that bring the arts (music, dance, drama and visual arts) into any classroom no matter the subject or grade level.

If you ever wondered how you could possibly top last year's conference or PD event, let Étienne help you with a dynamic keynote address especially tailored to your theme or current needs.

Contact Steven at www.rockyourclass.com

OTHER RESOURCES

Rock Your Class blog and website: www.rockyourclass.com

Instagram: @rockyourclass

Twitter: @rockyourclass

Étienne on Wikipedia:

Étienne Documentary "The Accidental Rockstar":

MORE FROM CODE BREAKER PUBLISHING

RISK TAKER:

Strengthen Your Courage, Blaze a New Trail and Ignite Your Students' Passions
Author: Brian Aspinall

CODE BREAKER:

15+ Ways To Get Started With Coding!
Increase Creativity, Remix Assessment And Develop A Class Of Coder Ninjas!
Author: Brian Aspinall

BLOCK BREAKER:

Building Knowledge And Amplifying Voice One Minecraft Block At A Time!
Author: Brian Aspinall

SCRATCHING THE SURFACE:

An Intro to Middle School Coding
Author: Brian Aspinall

THINK LIKE A CODER:

Connecting Computational Thinking to Everyday Activities
Co-author: Deanna Pecaski McLennan and Brian Aspinall

HALLWAY CONNECTIONS:

Autism and Coding
Author: Maggie Fay

GRACIE:

An Innovator Doesn't Complain About The Problem. She Solves It!
Author: Daphne McMenemy

www.ingramcontent.com/pod-product-compliance
Lightning Source LLC
Chambersburg PA
CBHW070913080526
44589CB00013B/1277